W9-CNA-133

Copyright © 2004 by Triumph Books. All rights reserved.

All photos and stories copyright AP Wide World except where otherwise noted.

Content packaged by Mojo Media, Inc.
Editor: Joe Funk
Creative Director: Jason Hinman
Senior Writer: Mark Murphy
Assistant Editor: Matt Springer

No part of this publication may be reproduced, stored in a retrieval system, or transmitted, in any form by any means, electronic, mechanical, photocopying, or otherwise, without prior written permission of the publisher, Triumph Books, 601 S. LaSalle St., Suite 500, Chicago, Illinois 60605.

This book is available in quantity at special discounts for your group or organization.
For further information, contact:

Triumph Books
601 S. LaSalle St.
Suite 500
Chicago, Illinois 60605
Phone: (312) 939-3330
Fax: (312) 663-3557

Printed in the United States of America

TIGER TRIUMPH

Contents

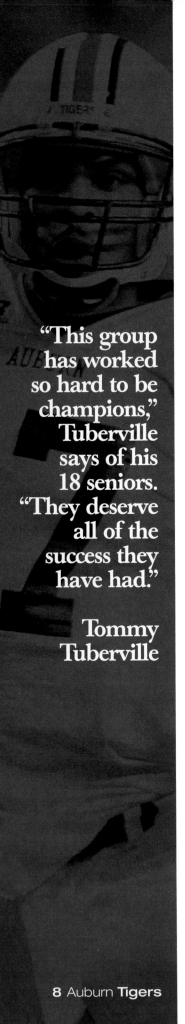

"This group
has worked
so hard to be
champions,"
Tuberville
says of his
18 seniors.
"They deserve
all of the
success they
have had."

Tommy
Tuberville

From Disappointment to Dominance

By Mark Murphy • Editor, *Inside the Auburn Tigers*

What a difference one year can make. Nobody knows that any better than the 2004 Auburn football Tigers.

Just one season after being accurately labeled as the biggest disappointment in the Southeastern Conference and one of the biggest disappointments in college football, the expectations were significantly lower this season, but the level of performance from the Tigers was decidedly higher.

Auburn finished its regular season unbeaten as the Tigers knocked off three Top 10 opponents while being only seriously in danger of losing one time. Offensively, defensively and in the kicking game, Coach Tommy Tuberville's Tigers showed no signs of weakness and the result was an 11-0 regular season record. Two weeks later the 12th victory was in the books when the Tigers knocked off the Tennessee Volunteers in a rematch at the annual SEC Football Championship Game at the Georgia Dome in Atlanta.

Along the way, Tuberville's Tigers put most of their opponents hopelessly behind by halftime. Veteran SEC watchers described the 2004 Tigers as one of the most impressive teams in Auburn history and one of the most complete teams to ever be crowned as the Southeastern Conference champion. It is difficult to come up with just a single reason why the Tigers were able to make the one-year transition from disappointment to dominance, however, it wasn't that difficult to predict if you carefully followed the transition from the end of the 2003 season to opening day of the 2004 schedule.

To understand the 2004 team's determination to succeed week after week, you have to go back to the summer of 2003 to gain perspective. Expectations for the 2003 season were high - very, very high. Talk of possible conference and national championships had been in high gear since the end of spring training. Talk of All-America honors and postseason awards were common, as Tuberville's fifth Auburn team appeared to have everything it needed for a run at glory.

Expectations were as high as they had been for a decade with lots of experienced players returning and improved depth plus big-play stars on both sides of the line of scrimmage. The Tigers were expected to win their first SEC title since a run of three in a row from 1987-1989 and some preseason forecasts had the Tigers as the team to beat for the national title.

However, those giddy predictions

Auburn's Courtney Taylor breaks the tackle of Tennessee's Jonathan Hefney after a reception on the first play of the Tigers 38-28 win in the SEC Championship game.

(above) Auburn coach Tommy Tuberville links arms with his players as they prance onto the field prior to the SEC championship game. (right) USC's Mike Williams bobbles a pass as Auburn's Carlos Rogers defends in what became a fateful game for both teams early in the 2003 season.

crashed on opening day and burned a week later in Atlanta at Grant Field, just a few miles north of the Georgia Dome where the Tigers would eventually celebrate a championship season with their second victory over Tennessee in 2004.

The celebration was particularly sweet for Tiger players and coaches who remembered the pain associated with the start of the 2003 season, that began with an ugly opening day loss with a packed house watching at Jordan-Hare Stadium and a national TV audience tuning in at home. The Tigers were awful offensively and the visitors from Southern Cal came to the heart of SEC country as an underdog and returned home with a dominating 23-0 victory that was nothing short of shocking to the Auburn Nation. (A year earlier the Trojans took a narrow 24-17 victory in Los Angeles, besting an Auburn team that was not as talented or experienced as the one the Trojans humbled in 2003. That victory over the Tigers helped jump-start USC on the road to a national championship season in the Associated Press poll.)

Back in Auburn, the Tigers tried to regroup as they prepared to renew what had become a dormant rivalry with former SEC member Georgia Tech. The Tigers had won their previous nine meetings vs. the Yellow Jackets, who opted out of the one-sided series following the 1987 game. Prevailing expectations were that despite playing miserably on offense in the opener against USC, the Tigers would march into Atlanta's Grant Field have no problem with the lightly regarded Atlantic Coast Conference team. However, in a setback even more discouraging and unexpected than the loss to Southern Cal, the Tigers were out of sync the entire game and soon out of hope for their dreams of a national title as the Yellow Jackets shocked the Tigers 17-3, prompting a wild celebration from Tech fans who stormed the field and tore down the goal posts.

While the Yellow Jackets danced on Grant Field, thousands of Auburn fans filed out of the stadium in disbelief while the players and coaches were hard-pressed trying to figure out why they were 0-2 with a team that should have been significantly more talented than the previous one, which had finished the year with nine wins, including two straight victories over Top 10 opponents to close the season.

To their credit, the 2003 Tigers did manage to regroup and make a serious run at the SEC West title. However, there was more disappointment just around the corner. In a game that would have put the Tigers in the driver's seat in the division, they suffered an agonizing home loss to an Eli Manning-led Ole Miss team in a game that Auburn had a chance to win until the clos-

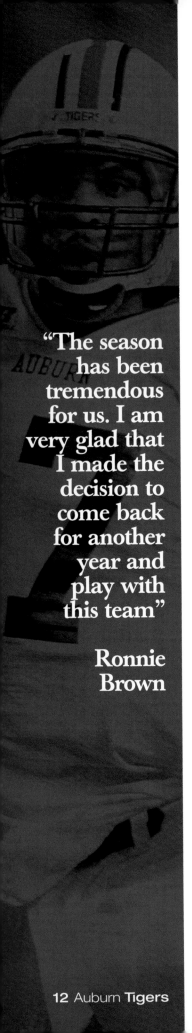

"The season has been tremendous for us. I am very glad that I made the decision to come back for another year and play with this team"

Ronnie Brown

ing seconds. However, a normally sure-handed uncovered receiver, sophomore Ben Obomanu, dropped the would-be winning TD pass in the end zone in the closing seconds, ending the team's hopes of salvaging the season with a conference title.

A week later, following an unimpressive performance in a 26-7 loss to Auburn's oldest rival, the Georgia Bulldogs, a chain of events was set in motion that laid the groundwork for a more prosperous 2004 season. That is when former Auburn University president Dr. William Walker made a behind the scenes move to try to replace the head coach with Louisville's Bobby Petrino, who had spent the 2002 season as Auburn's offensive coordinator before leaving to take his first post as a college head coach. However, word of what was supposed to be a secret meeting between Auburn University officials and Petrino at a small airport in southern Indiana leaked during the biggest week of each football season for Auburn players, coaches and fans: the annual intra-state showdown matching Auburn vs. Alabama.

While there had been discontent among Auburn fans about the season, that disappointment was nothing in comparison to the outrage directed towards Walker and a small group of board of trustees members for trying to sack the popular head coach. The fact that it happened as the Tigers were preparing for their arch-rival even angered Auburn fans who thought it was time for a new man to replace Tuberville.

Walker poured gasoline on the fire with contradictory statements about exactly what he and the others were doing in Indiana talking to Petrino. Meanwhile, Tuberville's Tigers defeated Alabama for a second straight year and instead of losing his job, his contract was renewed and sweetened after the university president's office was flooded with thousands of let-

ters, phone calls and emails telling him that Tuberville must stay.

However, the same fate did not await Walker. With the governor of the state of Alabama, Bob Riley, strongly suggesting that it was time for Walker to step aside and resign, that is exactly what happened.

Meanwhile, Tuberville remained calm and focused in the middle of the storm, prepared his team for a bowl game vs. Wisconsin and won a tremendous amount of respect from his players, assistant coaches and everyone connected with Auburn with how he handled himself throughout the ordeal. After the Tigers took care of business on the field with a 28-14 bowl victory in Nashville vs. the Badgers, Tuberville and his staff went into overtime mode trying to salvage a recruiting class that had been hit hard by the disappointment of the season and the controversy surrounding the botched attempt to fire the head coach.

While the coaches went to work lining up the next signee class for February, the players went to work in the weight room and in their offseason training program, more determined than ever to make the 2004 season memorable. Bolstered by a large senior class that included a variety of strong leaders, the seeds were sown.

Tuberville and his staff did a magnificent job on the recruiting trail salvaging the signee class, but the key recruiting job was done in keeping three of the team's star juniors on board for one more year and one more shot at chasing their dreams that had gone up in smoke back in September 2003. It was widely assumed that tailbacks Carnell Williams and Ronnie Brown would likely go pro, or least one would. However, at a press conference in January, just before the deadline to declare for the NFL draft, Williams and Brown were joined by cornerback Carlos Rogers. All

Tennessee defender Omar Gaither upends Auburn's Ronnie Brown in the SEC championship game.

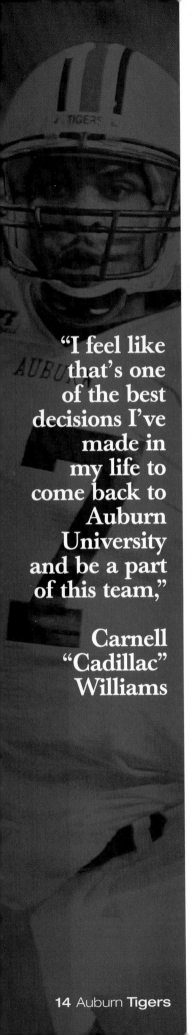

"I feel like that's one of the best decisions I've made in my life to come back to Auburn University and be a part of this team,"

Carnell "Cadillac" Williams

three announced they were returning to Auburn and planned to leave with a college degree and a senior season to remember. All three became key players in Auburn's run to the championship.

"I feel like that's one of the best decisions I've made in my life to come back to Auburn University and be a part of this team," says Williams, who broke the school record for career touchdowns set from 1982-85 by the legendary three-sport star, Bo Jackson. The Cadillac, who was named a first team All-American, leaves Auburn as the second leading rusher in school history, trailing only Jackson on a list filled with some of the best running backs in college football history.

"Just to be a part of what we're doing, the atmosphere and things like that has been great," Williams says. "I really like this football team. We are strong on offense, strong on defense and are really good with our special teams."

Williams would have likely been a first round draft pick, or close to it, following his junior year. That hasn't changed after another 1,000-yard plus senior season. Brown, meanwhile, has seen his stock as a pro prospect soar and he, too, is projected as a possible first round draft pick. The same is true for Rogers, who came back for a sensational senior year in which he was the top defensive back in the SEC. A steady stream of NFL scouts came to watch those three seniors perform in practices and games and all three are considered strong bets to be on NFL rosters in 2005.

Brown, who showed his skills as a running back and receiver as a change in offensive philosophy enabled the Tigers to use both Williams and Brown in the backfield at the same time, says he is ecstatic at how his senior season turned out. "When you make a decision like that, a big decision, you never want to feel like you have second guessed yourself, but since that point everything has been good," he says. "The season has been tremendous for us. I

am very glad that I made the decision to come back for another year and play with this team. We have a special group of seniors and a special team that has a been fun to be a part of."

Rogers, a rare four-year starter, had battled injuries in previous seasons, but he used the offseason prior to his senior campaign to add weight, strength and regain his good health. At six-foot-one, 200 pounds with quick feet, 40-yard dash speed in the 4.4 seconds range and lots of toughness, he became a lock-down cornerback who opposing offenses avoided like he was carrying a highly infectious disease. The only team to really test the

Tiger, his home-state Georgia Bulldogs, found out why the others left him alone as Rogers dominated UGA's star receivers and had a big performance stopping the run, too, on the way to being named the SEC and national defensive player of the week for his all-around performance in that game.

Like the tailbacks, Rogers says he is glad that he returned for his senior year instead of entering the NFL draft. "It is really good how this season has gone," he says. "That is something Carnell, Ronnie and I have been thinking about and talking about. I think coming back was a good decision for all of us. Last year we could have left and made some money, but to come back and be a part of this team is a good thing."

The next piece of the puzzle fell into place soon after the trio of seniors announced they were returning. Tuberville had made the decision that the one-year experiment of having highly regarded offensive line coach Hugh Nall run Petrino's offensive system, which had been productive in 2002, was not working. Petrino, who was hired by Louisville to be head coach after an impressive season as a coordinator at Auburn, had managed to make the Auburn offense work, even in a season in which the team was hit hard by injuries.

However, the following season the Petrino-style Auburn offense was not impressive without Petrino on hand to install the game plan each week and call the plays. Nall was asked to step down from his second role as offensive coordinator. He had other job offers, some very lucrative, but decided to stay at Auburn and concentrate on coaching his linemen while Tuberville found a new offensive coordinator, one with many years of experience on the job

Able to concentrate on coaching the guards, tackles and centers, Nall developed the best offensive front in the SEC and that played a major role in the 2004 team's success. Senior guard Danny Lindsey notes that he could see the makings of a special team being developed long before opening day of the 2004 season. "I knew in the spring how close our offensive line had gotten," Lindsey says. "We have grown even closer during the season. We are like blood brothers. Really, the whole team is a close group. We care about each other on and off the field and I think that is a major reason for our success. I have never been around a team as close as our team. It is amazing and unbelievable to be a part of something like this."

Prior to the start of spring practice, with input from Nall and the other assistant coaches, the decision was made to hire Al Borges to run the offense. Borges had built a reputation on the West Coast as a talented teacher of quarterbacks and a creative play caller, however, he was a stranger to the rough and tumble SEC. Auburn brought Borges in from Indiana University of the Big 10, where he was the offensive coordinator of an unimpressive team. That decision raised more than a few thousand pairs of eyebrows in the Auburn family.

Borges, a self-described football junkie, noted that he was immediately impressed by the talent on hand and the passion for football he found. Borges joked that he had been rescued from "football hell" at IU while landing in "football heaven" at Auburn.

While there was initial consternation as to why Tuberville didn't hire a more prominent offensive coordinator, that sentiment changed during spring drills as Borges won the respect of the players, coaches and fans with his "Gulf Coast Offense," a hybrid system that featured elements of the West Coast Offense that Borges had used at other coaching stops along with bits and pieces of different systems.

By the end of spring drills, it became obvious that the offense wasn't going to be the weak link in 2004, as had been the case in many of the big games a season earlier. However, there were major concerns about the defense, which lost five starters to the pros, including a pair of All-American linebackers, seniors Karlos Dansby and Dontarrious Thomas, plus its playmakers on the line of scrimmage. The way the offense pushed around the defense throughout spring drills, it looked like those concerns were well-founded.

However, instead of being discouraged, coordinator Gene Chizik and his defensive players found the challenge stimulating. By the end of spring drills, there were signs of progress being made. Although the team was missing its defensive stars and Chizik was publicly expressing major concerns about his group, he and the other defensive assistants knew the Tigers had a chance to be good because there was a lot of quality, young talent and depth on the defensive roster. The key was to mold it into a finely-tuned unit, which happened, albeit with some growing pains.

"I really think we improved a lot in the spring with the offense pushing us so hard," notes junior linebacker Travis Williams, who had quietly put together an impressive sophomore season in the shadow of Dansby and Thomas. Making the move from outside linebacker to the middle, Williams became leader of a group of undersized but extremely quick linebackers. Instead of being a team weakness as many feared, the linebackers turned out to be a team strength, just like Williams had predicted would be the case in preseason. The day before the SEC Championship Game, Tuberville proclaimed the 2004 linebackers were even better than the all-star 2003 group.

"People said we were too small, we were too inexperienced and we lost too many people to be good at linebacker or on defense, but we knew that wasn't true," Williams says. "We have got a lot of great athletes with lots of speed who know how to play the game and play together as a unit." The Tigers finished the regular season ranked number one nationally in scoring defense, a statistic that even the 2003 group couldn't match.

Williams notes that the players figured out early this season that something special was happening. "When we were in the locker room talking we always thought this year would be better than last year," the junior linebacker says. "I forgot who I was talking to, but it was a handful of us and I said, 'Man, maybe the voters picked us a year too soon as far as being number one.' We knew we had talent last year, but we knew that the

following year we'd have a lot more talent. And that has been the case. We are a much better team than we were last season."

Tuberville was upbeat as the Tigers emerged from a physical and intense spring training as a much better and more complete team than many suspected. His Tigers got through the 15 days of workouts with a minimal number of serious injuries and they met their goal of restructuring the offense.

In fact, they were actually way ahead of schedule, partly due to the impressive way that fifth-year senior quarterback Jason Campbell quickly learned Borges' system while playing for his fourth different offensive coordinator in college. Borges went out of his way to consistently praise Campbell, who completed a high percentage of passes in the scrimmages and made few mistakes, foreshadowing what would happen in the fall. "I have never had a quarterback learn my system as quickly as Jason did," says Borges.

After spring training, the offensive coordinator told NFL scouts that the under-appreciated senior was a prospect to watch. By the time the Tigers wrapped up the regular season undefeated with Campbell playing "as well as any quarterback in the country," according to Borges, the coach noted that there was zero doubt in his mind that the six-foot-five, 224-pounder with the big arm and a coach's son demeanor had developed into a high level pro prospect.

Tuberville says the memorable season couldn't have happened to a better group of football players, particularly the team's 18 seniors. "This group has worked so hard to be champions," he says. "They deserve all of the success they have had. This is a special group of football players who have done a great job leading this team. I am just happy to be along for the ride."

Auburn's Cole Bennett recovers a fumble by teammate Carnell Williams in the endzone in the first quarter as Tennessee's Jesse Mahelona piles on.

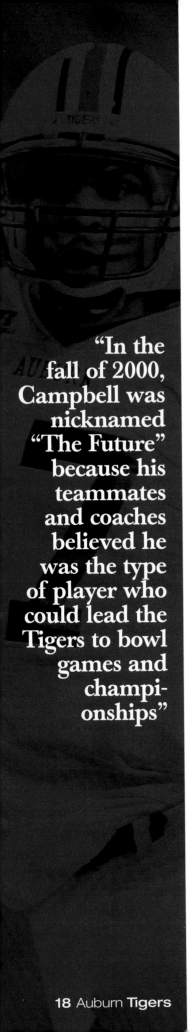

"In the fall of 2000, Campbell was nicknamed "The Future" because his teammates and coaches believed he was the type of player who could lead the Tigers to bowl games and championships"

No. 3 Auburn 38, No. 15 Tennessee 28
SEC Championship game December 4, 2004

MARK MURPHY, December 4, 2004

With the pressure on while playing on the biggest stage of his college career, "The Future" was now for quarterback Jason Campbell and his Auburn Tigers.

The former high school All-American was one of the key early recruits five years ago after Coach Tommy Tuberville came to Auburn from Ole Miss with the assignment of rebuilding a proud football program that had quickly hit the skids following a tumultuous 1998 season.

Campbell was part of Tuberville's first full signee class in February 2000. The two-sport star, who was a two-time All-State pick in football and basketball, had his choice of just about any college in the South and many others around the nation, but the coach's son from tiny Taylorsville, Miss., picked Auburn. Campbell, who played his final season as a graduate student, will leave the program for a shot at the NFL as one of the greatest quarterbacks in Auburn history.

Never was that more apparent than in the 2004 SEC Football Championship Game at the Georgia Dome in Atlanta. Campbell was named Most Valuable Player of the Game for a variety of reasons. First of all, he directed an Auburn attack that amassed 559 total yards of offense, the most in the league championship game's history, 57 more than a potent Tennessee offense led by Peyton Manning produced in 1997.

Campbell also passed for an SEC Championship Game and personal record 374 yards as he threw for three touchdowns while completing 27 of 35 passes.

His performance was also one for the Auburn record books as his total yardage of 431, including 57 net rushing yards, was the second most in Auburn history as well as a record for the league championship game.

While he was being redshirted in the fall of 2000, Campbell was nicknamed "The Future" because his teammates and coaches believed he was the type of player who could lead the Tigers to bowl games and championships, which is exactly how it played out even though his early development was uneven as he had to play under four different offensive coordinators and quarterback coaches in a four-year period.

Campbell's final collegiate position coach, Al Borges, has turned into a huge Jason Campbell fan. "This kid has played as well as any quarterback in the country all year," says Borges, who Campbell credits with being a major part of his success as a senior. Speaking over the cheers of thousands of Auburn fans in the Georgia Dome while

Auburn quarterback Jason Campbell looks downfield in the first quarter. Campbell connected on 27 of 35 passes for 374 yards and 3 touchdowns, and had 57 yards on 13 carries.

players and coaches hugged and celebrated in the end zone following their 38-28 SEC Championship Game victory over Tennessee, the offensive coordinator said he believed it was a shame that the senior quarterback didn't receive a call to go to New York City where the Heisman Trophy is presented annually to the nation's top college player.

"If we wanted to throw the ball 55 times a game, he would be up there in New York with the rest of them for the Heisman Trophy ceremony, but we don't play that way," Borges says. "Jason plays within our offense and does what we ask him to do. He just showed what he can do if we wanted to throw a lot of passes. Tennessee made it tough on us to run so we threw the ball more than we have been. When they start crowding the line of scrimmage that hard, like Tennessee was doing, you have to throw the ball over them and that is what we did."

Borges notes that Campbell understands the need to have a balanced attack and get the ball to fellow seniors Carnell "Cadillac" Williams and Ronnie Brown, the dual threat tailbacks who were a huge part of the team's run to a 12-0 record and the first SEC title for the Tigers since 1989.

All three are expected to be playing in the National Football League next season. Borges says there may have been doubts before Campbell's senior season about how good a pro prospect the 6-5, 224-pounder is, but his performance from game one to game 12 changed that.

"I am going to tell you why," Borges says. "When I talked to NFL scouts early in the year, and I talked to several guys, I said this kid really has a chance, but I want to take him through some games. I have got one foot on the soapbox then. I have got both up now. I am standing on top and screaming from the mountain tops because this kid can play in that league because has got what it takes to play in that league - he can pass.

"He is also athletic enough to get out of jams. He has got enough sense to handle any offense. God knows he has proven that. You tell me what is wrong with him and I will give you an argument against it. I don't see anything wrong with him at this point."

Auburn head coach Tommy Tuberville notes that he is not the least bit surprised how Campbell has played as a senior. "Jason Campbell has always been a good quarter-

Jason Campbell reaches for the ball after a fumble. Campbell shook off the third quarter turnover and provided senior leadership and good decision-making throughout the game.

back. The problem, I told everybody, is when he started for us a few years ago the supporting cast wasn't nearly as strong as it is today. We have a lot better offensive line, the receivers are better and the running backs are better. Al Borges came in and put some imagination into the offense."

Speaking in his postgame press conference following a second victory over Tennessee this season, Tuberville declared his senior is a special player. "There is not a better one in the country. I see all of these quarterbacks going to New York for the Heisman. There is going to be one guy who is not on that bus who ought to be there."

Tuberville says that Campbell is just as good a person as he is a football player and a key member of what the coach calls a special team featuring a special group of seniors. "I couldn't be any more prouder of the guy for what he stands for and what he has done," Tuberville says. "He has many years in front of him after playing the last game here."

Tennessee head coach Phil Fulmer, who also watched up close and personally as Campbell carved up his defense during a 34-10 victory over the Vols on Oct. 2nd in Knoxville, notes that he was impressed with the quarterback and the entire team. Fulmer's 1998 Vols ran the table just like Auburn did in the SEC and were able to win the national title. Comparing that UT team with the 2004 Tigers, Fulmer says, "They run the football well and they can make big plays in the passing game. Jason Campbell, I was just looking at his numbers, and that's incredible what he just did statistically. They have got enough good players to play with anybody in the country. On any given day, they can beat Oklahoma or USC."

Unfortunately for Campbell, Tuberville and the Tigers, the opportunity to play in the BCS national championship game at the Orange Bowl in Miami didn't happen because the teams that started the season at the top of the rankings, Southern Cal and Oklahoma, managed to stay unbeaten, too. That sent the Tigers to the Sugar Bowl for a game vs. ACC champion Virginia Tech.

Campbell's fellow senior and co-captain for the SEC Championship Game, defensive end Bret Eddins, says it isn't right that the Tigers didn't get an opportunity to play in the BCS national title matchup. "We won by good margins in every game this year except for one and we play in the Southeastern Conference," he points out. "If that is

Carnell "Cadillac" Williams strikes a classic pose as he puts the straight-arm on Tennessee's Jonathan Wade.

"To win this way means a lot. I think it shows the composure of this team the way we stuck together through the tough times."

Jason Campbell

Auburn coach Tommy Tuberville, left, is hugged by quarterback Jason Campbell.

not enough to get us into the BCS championship game, I don't know what is."

Campbell, who finished just 14 yards short of the school record for total offense set by QB Dameyune Craig vs. Army in the 1996 Independence Bowl, hit the big play of the game in the third quarter. Although Auburn had dominated statistically in the first half, the Tigers led just 21-7. After the Vols rallied to tie the game at 21-21 with an 80-yard run by Gerald Riggs with 6:05 in the third quarter, the underdogs from Knoxville had gained the momentum and were looking for the big upset. However, Campbell and his teammates on offense did something about that immediately.

Six plays later the Tigers were back on top 28-21 as they moved 85 yards for the score. The big one was a 53-yard touchdown pass to junior speedster Devin Aromashodu, who outran the UT secondary and caught the ball in stride inside the five-yard line and ran in for the score.

"On the pass to Devin, we felt like we could get them in one on one coverage," Campbell says. "We had been throwing a lot of things at them underneath. We thought it

was a great time to try them out deep and Devin did a great job on the play. He got downfield in a hurry."

Auburn added a 22-yard John Vaughn field goal with 11:46 to play after an 11-play, 39-yard drive to stretch the lead to 31-21. However, the Vols kept the heat on with a five-play, 80-yard drive that was capped by a nine-yard run by Gerald Riggs, who had a big night with 182 rushing yards on just 11 carries. His rushing total was the second highest in SEC Championship Game history.

With the pressure on the Auburn offense again, the Tigers matched that TD with an 80-yard drive of their own on just six plays. Again Campbell came through with the big play, a 43-yard pass to Ben Obomanu. When Campbell notices that the defense jumps offsides, the Tigers have a play in which they go for the home run as the wide receiver on the outside runs a fly pattern toward the end zone. Once again, the ball was right on target and the Tigers were able to put the game away after their fifth touchdown.

Tuberville says the defense was able to make adjustments to the running plays that were hurting the Tigers in the third quarter. After that, the Vols again struggled to move the football. Auburn probably could have scored again late in the game, but elected to let time run out after making a first down at the Vol seven-yard line.

Earlier in the game, Tennessee was the team that needed to make adjustments. The Tigers scored more quickly than any team in SEC Championship Game history, moving 86 yards on four plays to take a 7-0 lead. Campbell hit Courtney Taylor on a 56-yard catch and run to start the drive. On the third play, he hit tight end Cooper Wallace on a pass play for 21 yards to the UT four. On first and goal, Carnell Williams ran toward the goal line, lost the football and it was recovered by reserve tight end Cole Bennett at the 13:24 mark for the score.

The Vols couldn't move on their first possession and Auburn got its second chance starting on its 34-yard line. This time it took the Tigers nine plays to put the ball into the end zone. They started with passes of 13 yards to Brown and 15 to Obomanu. Williams, who had a 14-yard run on the drive, scored the touchdown on a five-yarder around left end. The Cadillac rushed for 100 yards on 19 carries to lead the Tigers on the ground.

Tennessee couldn't manage a first down on its next possession either, but finally forced a three and out and got good field position when normally steady Kody Bliss punted the ball out of bounds for just 15 yards. UT took over at its own 45, but couldn't move again. However, Auburn had another three and out on offense and followed it with another miscue from Bliss. This one was costly as he bobbled a slightly high snap and fell on it for a 22-yard loss, putting the underdogs in great field position at the Auburn 14.

It took the Vols four plays to score as Cedric Houston jumped over the top at right guard for a two-yard TD run on the final play of the first quarter. That was just the second rushing touchdown the Tigers had allowed all season.

Auburn responded with its third long drive of the game, marching 80 yards in 12 plays. Two big plays early in the drive set up the touchdown. Campbell hit Taylor on a 25-yard pass play and then ran for 28 yards around left end after standing deep in the pocket looking to hit a long pass play. The TD came on a four-yard pass to Taylor, who was uncovered in the end zone as the UT defense played the run as Campbell made a good run fake before throwing the pass.

Tennessee got its second first down of the half on its next possession, but Auburn's defense held again and the Tigers took over at their own 13 following a 50-yard punt. The Tigers got the ball with 6:21 left and moved all the way to Tennessee 11 yard line after converting a pair of fourth down plays. The first was on a quarterback sneak on fourth and an inch at the UT 49. The second was an 18-yard pass to Obomanu on fourth and six at the UT 29 with 24 seconds left in the half.

After calling the second timeout, Campbell tried to hit Taylor in the end zone again. However, the ball was deflected by linebacker Omar Gaither and Corey Campbell intercepted in the end zone. At the half, the Tigers held a 303-29 advantage in total offense. They had 17 first downs to two for the Vols. Campbell hit 18-24 passes for 217 yards and had another 51 yards on seven carries. Tennessee rallied offensively to finish with 297 total yards to Auburn's 559, but the Tigers had answers for everything the Vols threw at them.

To win this way means a lot," Campbell says. "I think it shows the composure of this team the way we stuck together through the tough times."

It was hard to find tough times during the 2004 season for Campbell and his Tigers as they became the first team in school history to go 12-0 as they won Auburn's sixth SEC football championship in as impressive style as any team in the school's long and successful football history.

	Auburn	Tennessee
First Downs	31	9
3rd Down Efficiency	8-14-57%	2-9-22%
4th Down Efficiency	2-3-67%	0-1-0%
Total Net Yards	559	297
Net Yards Rushing	185	228
Net Yards Passing	374	69
Penalties-yards	4-20	12-95
Time of Possession	39:31	20:29

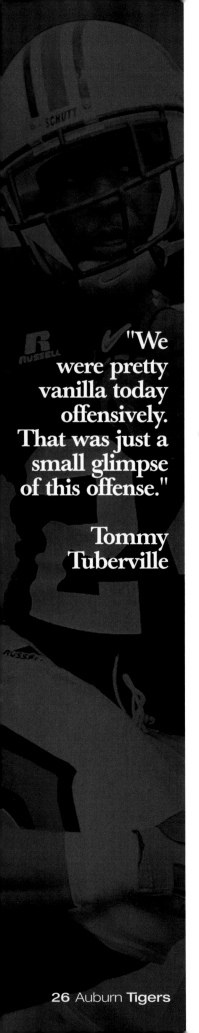

"We were pretty vanilla today offensively. That was just a small glimpse of this offense."

Tommy Tuberville

No. 17 Auburn 31, Louisiana-Monroe 0

September 4, 2004

JOHN ZENOR, September 4, 2004

Auburn's offense produced points and the no- name defense didn't allow any, a flip-flop from last season's awful opener.

Jason Campbell passed for two touchdowns and Carnell Williams ran for 103 yards as the 17th-ranked Tigers unveiled a new offense in a 31-0 victory over Louisiana-Monroe on Saturday.

The Tigers' West Coast offense sputtered at times but still fared better than in last year's opening shutout defeat to Southern California that set the stage for a disappointing season.

"It's good to come out here and have a little warmup game and see where we're at," Auburn safety Junior Rosegreen said. "Last year, I think we just jumped into the fire with no time to warmup."

It wasn't quite the offensive showcase Auburn fans were hoping for against the overmatched Sun Belt Conference team, but the Tigers saved much of their playbook for Southeastern Conference play.

"We were pretty vanilla today offensively," coach Tommy Tuberville said. "That was just a small glimpse of this offense."

It was a bigger glimpse of Williams, who played into the fourth quarter but never broke a long gain.

He carried 23 times and caught a 9-yard touchdown pass but was mostly contained by a swarming Louisiana-Monroe defense geared toward stopping the run.

"They were playing hard out there," receiver Courtney Taylor said. "Carnell came to the sideline and he was like, 'Hey, I break away from one and they come at me with two or three more.'"

Auburn's defense had to replace five starters in its front seven, including most of its stars, but still managed its first shutout since the second game two years ago against Western Carolina. Starting cornerback Montae Pitts was also suspended for the game for violation of team policy before the game, but it didn't matter in this one.

The Tigers improved to 12-0 against Sun Belt teams, allowing few yards after the catch against the Indians' short passing game.

"We really went in with new faces, so we really don't have an identity on defense," linebacker Travis Williams said. "Right now, we're trying to find our identity."

Louisiana-Monroe's Steven Jyles was 16-of-22 passing for only 96 yards with an interception. The Indians had only one pass play over 11 yards, and that 22-yarder came late.

Louisiana-Monroe's Cash Mouton knocks the ball away from Auburn's Courtney Taylor.

(left) Auburn running back Carnell Willaims avoids the attempted tackle of Louisiana-Monroe's Jason Schule during the first half. (above) Auburn's Ronnie Brown (23) is stopped after a first-down run by Louisiana Monroe's Shelton Williams (23) and Mikkal Henry.

Williams returned it 42 yards across midfield but the drive ended in the first of two missed field goals for the Indians, who also lost their last five games in 2003.

Louisiana-Monroe found a few more positives than from last year's 70-3 defeat that was a low point in a 1-11 season.

"Games against ranked teams will make you or break you," said Jyles, who missed last year's game because of a death in the family. "We came in to see what we had as a team this season. It lets us know where we stand. If we can compete with Auburn, we can win our conference and compete with any team."

Auburn revamped an offense that didn't produce a touchdown in the first two games last season but it's clearly still geared toward the run. The Tigers ran 41 times for 194 yards.

"We didn't hit on all cyliners on the offense at all times, but it was a steady game," Tuberville said. "We got the job done."

"I don't know if it was how well their defense played or how poorly we played," Louisiana-Monroe coach Charlie Weatherbie said. "It was probably a combination.

"They manhandled us up front."

The Tigers showed a little more ability to get the ball downfield, including Campbell's 32-yard touchdown pass to Devin Aromashodu early in the third quarter after the defender tripped.

Campbell was 11-of-18 for 110 yards but lost a fumble and threw an interception, splitting time with redshirt freshman Brandon Cox. Cox ran for a 14-yard touchdown after hitting Taylor for a 39- yarder on his first pass, the longest gain for either team.

Ronnie Brown also ran for a 30-yard touchdown in the third quarter.

New Auburn coordinator Al Borges' offense scored on its first three possessions to build a 17-0 lead and was marching again when Campbell was picked off by Shelton Williams deep in Louisiana- Monroe territory after getting hit as he threw.

	Louisiana-Monroe	Auburn
First Downs	12	21
3rd Down Efficiency	2-12-17%	9-15-60%
4th Down Efficiency	2-2-100%	0-0-0%
Total Net Yards	239	380
Net Yards Rushing	140	194
Net Yards Passing	99	186
Penalties-yards	7-75	6-60
Time of Possession	30:11	29:49

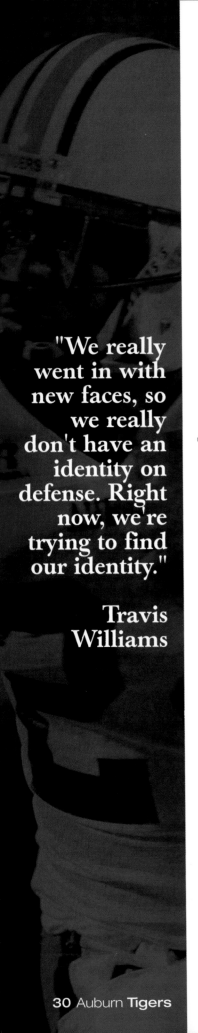

"We really went in with new faces, so we really don't have an identity on defense. Right now, we're trying to find our identity."

Travis Williams

No. 18 Auburn 43, Mississippi State 14

September 11, 2004

JOEDY McCreary, September 11, 2004

Auburn's Cadillac enjoyed another drive through Mississippi State's defense.

Carnell Williams ran for 122 yards and two touchdowns to lead the 18th-ranked Tigers past Mississippi State 43-14 on Saturday.

The flashy slasher nicknamed "Cadillac," who rushed for a school- record six touchdowns last year against the Bulldogs, surpassed the 100-yard rushing mark for the second time this season, and the Tigers dominated the line of scrimmage on both sides of the ball.

Ronnie Brown, the Tigers' other tailback, ran for 147 yards.

"We were in the zone—it didn't matter what down or distance," Williams said. "Me and Ronnie get a lot of ink, but (the offensive line) deserves the credit."

Jason Campbell threw two of his three touchdown passes to Anthony Mix, and Auburn (2-0, 1-0 Southeastern Conference) scored on three of its first four possessions to give Sylvester Croom a loss in the first SEC game for the league's first black head football coach.

Auburn won its fourth straight in the series, the last three by an average of nearly 30 points, and this time the Tigers used a punishing ground game that took advantage of poor tackling and mental mistakes by Mississippi State (1-1, 0-1), which entered with the No. 1 defense in the SEC after suffocating Tulane 28-7 last week.

"I thought we would tackle better," Croom said. "Maybe I'm a little bit naive about that."

Auburn's 283 rushing yards were more than three times the Bulldogs' rushing total, and the Tigers gained 465 total yards.

As long as the Tigers' tailback-by-committee system keeps working, coach Tommy Tuberville said he sees no reason to tinker with it.

"If we can continue to rotate them like we did today, I think we are going to be successful," Tuberville said.

Williams scored on runs of 1 and 3 yards. Brown's 59-yard run in the second quarter set up Campbell's second TD pass of the game.

"It's still in our game plan to play smash-mouth football," Brown said. "That's never going to change. ... Anytime two backs rush for over 100 yards, it's tremendous."

Campbell finished 8-for-17 for 139 yards with touchdown passes of 5 and 58 yards to Mix and 25 yards to Ben Obomanu. For the second straight week, Auburn kept things simple offensively.

"We didn't throw much (because) we just wanted to grind it out," Tuberville said.

Auburn quarterback Brandon Cox (12) fumbles as he is sacked by Mississippi State defensive lineman Avery Hannibal (51) in the fourth quarter. Mississippi State recovered the fumble and scored during the next series of downs.

Omarr Conner was 16-of-26 for 113 yards in his second start at quarterback for Mississippi State. The former high school quarterback played receiver last season.

Backup Kyle York threw two touchdown passes to Jason Husband in the closing minutes.

Croom has enjoyed far better days against Auburn. The Tuscaloosa, Ala., native and former Alabama standout is 10-5 as a player and coach against Auburn, and is rebuilding a struggling Mississippi State team that won eight games over the past three seasons.

"We have a long way to go," Croom said. "Our entire football team is a still a work in progress."

Auburn backs give Mississippi State a lesson in experience

JOEDY McCREARY, September 12, 2004

Auburn's tandem of tailbacks reminded Mississippi State just how far the rebuilding Bulldogs have to go.

Carnell Williams sidestepped around–and Ronnie Brown zipped through–Mississippi State's defense with ease during the Tigers' 43-14 rout on Saturday.

Williams ran for 122 yards and two touchdowns while Brown had 147 yards rushing behind an experienced Auburn offensive line that overwhelmed the Bulldogs' younger defensive front and sprung the Tigers' tailbacks for long gains.

"We were in the secondary most of the time and had a full head of steam," Brown said.

Mississippi State's miserable day started right away.

Brown set the tone with a 13-yard run on the first play from scrimmage. Two plays later, Williams ran for 10 yards. In all, Auburn had four runs of at least 10 yards on its opening drive.

"We were consistent all day long," Auburn

"We didn't hit on all cyliners on the offense at all times, but it was a steady game. We got the job done."

Tommy Tuberville

Auburn's offensive line blasted spacious holes for the Tigers' tailbacks.

Williams ran for 78 yards in the first quarter, and the Tigers went up 14-0 on their first two possessions.

"I knew they could run the football," Croom said. "I didn't expect us to totally shut then down. When they can run it like that, they can do anything they want."

Meanwhile, Auburn's defense had Mississippi State's running game out of whack. The Bulldogs didn't advance inside the Tigers' 30 in the first half. Auburn led 21-0 at halftime.

"From pre-snap penalties to lining up wrong, we just did things you're not supposed to," receiver Will Prosser said.

Mississippi State rushed for 11 yards in the first half and finished with 81.

Jerious Norwood, the SEC's offensive player of the week after running for 112 yards last week, had just eight at halftime and finished with 41 yards.

(above) Auburn running back Carnell Williams (24) sprints past a Mississippi defender on his way to a 4th quarter 29-yard touchdown run. (right) Auburn defensive tackle Jay Ratliff (83) rushes Mississippi State quarterback Omarr Conner (14) into a first quarter pass.

coach Tommy Tuberville said. "We got the momentum pretty quick and scored 14 points, and they could not stop us."

Mississippi State's defense was consistent, too—consistently porous.

Showing little resemblance to the group that smothered Tulane and entered No. 1 in the SEC, Mississippi State (1-1, 0-1) allowed 283 rushing yards—more than three times what the Bulldogs gained on the ground—and gave up 465 total yards.

"I do not think that we gave our best out there," Bulldogs coach Sylvester Croom said. "I do not even know that if we had given our best that we would have won. But I know that is not as good as we can play."

Jason Campbell threw three touchdown passes, two to Anthony Mix, and was 8-of-17 for 139 yards. But with Williams and Brown running strong behind a line with two seniors and two juniors, the Tigers didn't need anything fancy.

"We still haven't run much of the West Coast offense," Tuberville said. "If we're going to win this game, we'll do it running the football."

Auburn (2-0, 1-0 Southeastern Conference) won its fourth straight in the series, the last three by an average of nearly 30 points. Last year, Williams rushed for a school-record six touchdowns against the Bulldogs.

Brown got into the act this time against a Mississippi State defensive front which started just one senior.

"Mississippi State looked (on film) like they would come off the ball a little better than I thought they did," Auburn lineman Danny Lindsey said. "Having (Williams and Brown) as backs, we never know which one is back there because they come in and out. If we do our job up front, they are going to make something happen."

	Auburn	Mississippi State
First Downs	21	13
3rd-Down Efficiency	4-9-44%	7-17-41%
4th-Down Efficiency	1-1-100%	1-2-50%
Total net yards	465	271
Net yards rushing	283	81
Net yards passing	182	190
Penalties-yards	6-45	6-50
Time of Possession	26:32	33:28

Auburn center Jeremy Ingle (67) battles Mississippi State defensive lineman Corey Clark (97) as running back Carnell Williams (24) sprints to a second quarter 10-yard gain.

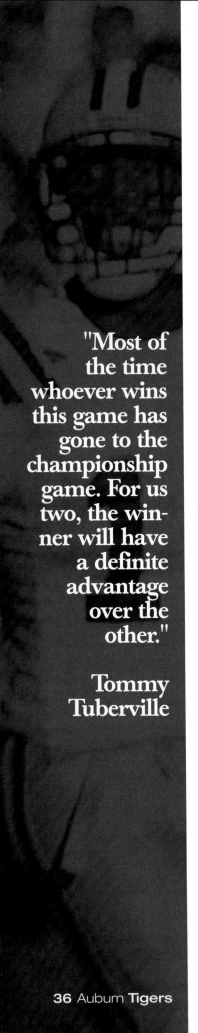

"Most of the time whoever wins this game has gone to the championship game. For us two, the winner will have a definite advantage over the other."

Tommy Tuberville

No. 14 Auburn 10, No. 5 LSU 9

September 18, 2004

LSU-Auburn rivalry could get another chapter: The Hurricane Game

JOHN ZENOR, September 18, 2004

Auburn and LSU have played several nickname games in recent years: The Fire Game. The Interception Game. The Cigar Game.

The latest entry might be The Hurricane Game.

Saturday's high-stakes matchup between No. 14 Auburn and No. 5 LSU is in limbo because of Hurricane Ivan. The storm plowed into Alabama and Louisiana and left concerns about safety, travel plans and available support personnel.

Auburn officials will likely decide Friday morning whether to reschedule the afternoon game.

Hurricane Ivan already has forced the postponement of two Top 25 games. No. 10 California was scheduled to play at Southern Mississippi on Thursday night and No. 24 Louisville was slated to play Tulane at the Superdome in New Orleans on Saturday.

Auburn-LSU is one of two heavyweight contests in the Southeastern Conference on Saturday. No. 11 Florida is at No. 13 Tennessee, with the winner clearing a major hurdle toward an Eastern division title.

In other Top 25 action on Saturday, No. 1 Southern California is at BYU; No. 2 Oklahoma plays host to Oregon; and No. 3 Georgia faces Marshall, which gave Ohio State a scare last week. The ninth-ranked Buckeyes are at North Carolina State.

No. 4 Miami gets a bit of a break after its big win over Florida State by hosting Louisiana Tech, while the eighth-ranked Seminoles also step down in competition with a home game against UAB.

No. 7 West Virginia looks to break a four-game losing streak to No. 21 Maryland in a Big East vs. Atlantic Coast Conference matchup.

Elsewhere, No. 12 Virginia hosts Akron; No. 15 Utah is at Utah State; No. 16 Iowa visits Arizona State; No. 17 Michigan plays host to San Diego State; and No. 19 Fresno State, coming off an impressive win, plays Portland State.

Two ranked Big Ten teams face potentially tricky road games with No. 20 Wisconsin at Arizona and No. 22 Minnesota visiting Colorado State.

No. 23 Boise State is at UTEP and No. 25 Memphis, playing its first game as a ranked team, is at Arkansas State.

As usual, the Auburn-LSU rivalry combines a dramatic story line with SEC title

Auburn's Brett Eddins sacks Louisiana State quarterback Marcus Randell (12) in the third quarter.

Auburn's Courtney Taylor catches a pass for a touchdown late in the fourth quarter.

implications. The two Tigers are the favorites to win the West.

"They compete hard against us and that's what makes a rivalry great," LSU defensive end Marcus Spears said. "No matter what the situation is when we play each other we want to play our best game. It's just important for us to play well.

"It's a great game, a great atmosphere to be a part of."

Often the subplots aren't bad, either.

In 1994, Auburn returned three of its five fourth-quarter interceptions for touchdowns to rally for a 30-26 win.

In 1996, the Auburn Sports Arena burned just outside Jordan-Hare Stadium, smoke billowing above the bleachers. LSU won 19-15 as Auburn missed three field goals and an extra point.

In 1999, Auburn punctuated a 41-7 win at Baton Rouge with coach Tommy Tuberville and his players firing up victory cigars on the game. Before the game, they danced on the eye of the tiger at midfield.

The teams have played their share of clunkers, too. Since 1998, the average margin of victory has been 20.5 points with blowouts on both sides.

"Most of the time whoever wins this game has gone to the championship game," said Tuberville, who promised he would hold off on a celebratory stogie until he gets home if his team wins. "For us two, the winner will have a definite advantage over the other.

"We all want to play it, and we'd love to keep going on a regular schedule and hopefully this thing will blow over and we can play on Saturday."

Last season, Auburn (2-0, 1-0) entered the game with a five-game winning streak and 4-0 league record after stumbling in its first two games. LSU jumped out 21-0 in the first quarter and shut Auburn out for 54 minutes of a 31-7 win.

Auburn lost its next two conference games while LSU (2-0) went on to win a share of the national championship.

Linebacker Travis Williams doesn't rate this rivalry up there with Alabama or Georgia, but last year's game does ratchet it up in his mind.

"It's a little different, because they kind of handed it to us last year," Williams said. "We've been thinking about this for a whole year."

Auburn had won the previous meeting by the same score as last year's game.

"They came out and played hard and had something to prove," Auburn receiver Courtney Taylor said. "Now,

I feel like it's back on us so they're saying, 'Hey, it's y'all's turn.'

"We're going to take the initiative and we're going to try to throw the first punch at them Saturday."

LSU coach Nick Saban isn't necessarily treating this as just another game but also doesn't want his team swept up in the hype.

"We need to play these games one game at a time, and we need to become a better football team with every experience that we have," Saban said. "That will be the focus of what we try to do in this game."

No. 14 Auburn 10, No. 5 LSU 9

JOHN ZENOR, September 19, 2004

The ball finally got to Courtney Taylor, the flag rescued John Vaughn and No. 14 Auburn proved itself an SEC contender.

Jason Campbell hit Taylor for a 16-yard touchdown pass with 1:14 to play and Auburn got two chances to kick the winning extra point in a 10-9 victory over No. 5 LSU Saturday.

"It was coming so slow, I was just saying, 'Come on, get here ball," said Taylor, whose first career touchdown catch proved huge.

Then, he watched in shock as LSU was nearly saved again by a missed extra point. Vaughn's first PAT attempt went wide left after a low snap, but Ronnie Prude was called for a personal foul, giving Auburn (3-0, 2-0 Southeastern Conference) another shot.

"(There) couldn't possibly be a bigger relief than that little yellow thing on the ground," Vaughn said.

Vaughn drilled his next try through the uprights with holder Sam Rives saving another bad snap for Auburn's 191st consecutive made PAT. It prevented a repeat of LSU's season opener when Oregon State's Alexis Serna missed his third extra point of the game in overtime for a 22-21 LSU victory.

LSU's Ryan Gaudet instead missed the kick following LSU's touchdown on a brilliant opening drive that was definitely not a sign of things to come.

"That's a really tough game for our players," LSU coach Nick Saban said. "We just had a lot of opportunities we squandered."

Auburn's final drive provided just about the only offensive dramatics. Campbell led a 12-play, 59-yard march that milked most of the remaining 6:38 off the clock.

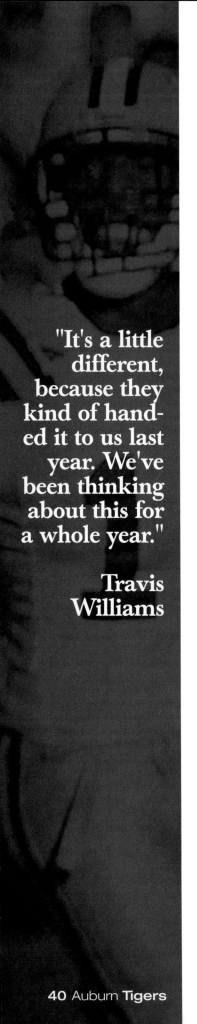

"It's a little different, because they kind of hand-ed it to us last year. We've been thinking about this for a whole year."

Travis
Williams

Ronnie Brown had a 20-yard run and Campbell and Taylor did the rest, including a 14-yard pass on fourth-and-12 from the 28.

The score came on third-and-12, with Campbell finding Taylor in the back of the end zone. Taylor knelt on his right knee in quiet celebration after the score and many Auburn fans hung around after the game, far less quietly.

"It was a huge sigh of relief," said Campbell, who was 16-of-27 for 170 yards and no interceptions. "We knew if we kept plugging, something would happen."

Taylor wasn't just worrying about the ball getting to him.

"At the same time, I was praying, 'Please God, let me catch this ball,'" he said.

LSU (2-1, 0-1), which had its 10-game winning streak snapped, moved into Auburn territory behind redshirt freshman quarterback JaMarcus Russell. But his final pass deflected off Early Doucet into the hands of Auburn's Junior Rosegreen with 8 seconds left.

"It's a tough way to lose a game," Saban said. "And it's a tough way to end a game."

LSU pounded Auburn 31-7 last season in Baton Rouge, a crippling blow to a team that had SEC championship aspirations that now seem far more realistic.

"All we had to do was just keep giving our offense chances to score," Rosegreen said. "It feels real good because last year they took our heart. All week, we've been thinking about payback."

LSU's shaky offense _ with Russell and Marcus Randall rotating _ finally caught up with the defending BCS champions.

The game's status was in doubt until Friday morning because of Hurricane Ivan, which affected both Alabama and Louisiana but didn't prevent a sellout crowd (87,451).

They were treated to a pair of defenses that allowed few yards and no points after the first 17 minutes in a stalemate that last-ed nearly to the end.

The previous six meetings had been decided by an average of 20.5 points.

With both offenses playing conservative-ly, it was the defenses that tried to turn the momentum with big stops late in the third quarter.

LSU drove to Auburn's 33 but got pushed back 30 yards by penalties and a sack.

Auburn moved to the LSU 3 but Campbell's pass to Anthony Mix in the end zone fell incomplete on fourth down.

"We were just fighting for field position, because we knew we could make a 50-yard drive," Auburn coach Tommy Tuberville said. "We just kept fighting and fighting to get that field position."

Randall directed a nearly flawless open-ing drive, moving LSU 80 yards on 14 plays and hitting Dwayne Bowe for a 9-yard touchdown pass. LSU only completed one more pass before the half and Randall was 0-for-3 the rest of the way.

"After that opening drive, we just said we weren't going to give them anything else," Auburn's Stanley McGlover said.

Auburn then drove to LSU's 5-yard line but settled for Vaughn's 29-yard field goal. The only other scoring until the final min-utes was Chris Jackson's 42-yard field goal for LSU early in the second quarter.

Taylor becoming Auburn's go-to receiver

JOHN ZENOR, September 20, 2004

A basketball star and state champion high jumper in high school, Courtney Taylor is used to athletic success.

And that has given the wideout for ninth-ranked Auburn something valuable.

"It's a cocky attitude," he said. "You've got to have some cockiness in you to play receiver. It just comes down to the

---

Auburn quarterback Jason Campbell is sacked by Louisiana State's Lionel Turner.

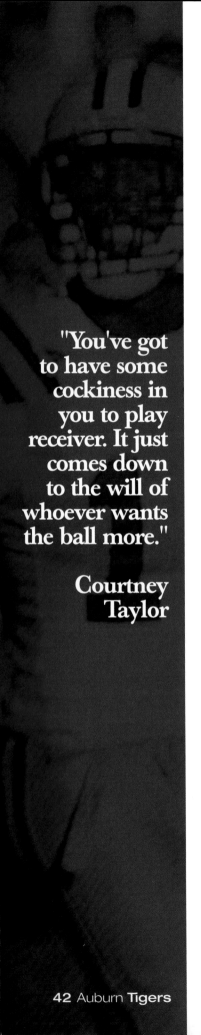

"You've got to have some cockiness in you to play receiver. It just comes down to the will of whoever wants the ball more."

Courtney
Taylor

will of whoever wants the ball more."

But, even with the previous success, it's taken some time for the loquacious Taylor to gain his swagger on the football field.

But he's got it now, and his performance Saturday against No. 13 LSU showed why.

Taylor made two key catches on Auburn's game-winning drive in a 10-9 victory.

First, he gained 14 yards on a fourth-and-12 to keep the drive alive. Then, on third-and-12 with 1:14 to play, Taylor caught a 16- yard touchdown pass from Jason Campbell to give Auburn the win.

"He's come a long way in a year," Auburn coach Tommy Tuberville said. "He didn't have a lot of confidence last year. He's a good athlete and if you put a basketball in his hands he'd have a lot more confidence than he would a football up to this point.

"He dominated when he was in high school (in basketball). Being a football player, it's taken him a little while to understand the speed of the game."

The Tigers need Taylor to start understanding.

The team's receivers were viewed by some as a weak link this season, plagued by dropped passes. But with Taylor, who has eight catches for a team-high 126 yards, and Anthony Mix emerging as bona fide threats, Auburn has a complement to its vaunted running game.

"This kid has a lot of ability," offensive coordinator Al Borges said of Taylor. "I told you if there was a player that would surprise everybody by the end of the season it would be him. I hope this game was a little bit of a coming out party for him because he has a world of ability."

Auburn receivers coach Greg Knox noted that competitiveness on the basketball court, too.

"I saw that during the recruiting part of it while watching him play basketball," Knox said. "If the game was close, he wanted the ball in his hands. He's always been a competitive young man."

Taylor also had another big catch that

was far less noticed on Saturday. After LSU consumed nearly seven minutes on its opening drive, Auburn failed to gain anything on its first two plays and was about to have to put its weary defense right back on the field.

Instead, Campbell hit Taylor on a 17-yarder for a first down.

Cornerback Junior Rosegreen said Taylor predicted he was going to have a big game.

"He told me before the game even started, 'I'm going to take this game over,'" Rosegreen said.

He was a running quarterback at Carrollton High School, where he also averaged 20 points and 10 rebounds for the basketball team.

Even without any experience at receiver, Taylor started five games last season and was second on the team as a redshirt freshman with 34 catches for 379 yards. But he had no touchdowns.

"I thought I would be scoring every game," Taylor admitted.

The Tigers hope from now on that will be the case.

Russo on Football: Kicking it away

RALPH D. RUSSO, September 19, 2004

Even the chip shots have become an adventure.

With parity spreading, the difference between contending for a title and playing in the Alamo Bowl can be just a few points. Kickers may be more important than ever.

Three weeks into the college football season, kickers have provided many of the most memorable moments--both good and bad.

Defending BCS champ LSU has been at the center of the kicking follies.

The Tigers opened the season with the luckiest of victories, gift- wrapped by Oregon State redshirt freshman kicker Alexis Serna.

In his first game as the Beavers' starter,

Serna missed three extra points. The final shank came in overtime with a chance to tie. LSU avoided a loss that could have derailed its hopes of a repeat.

For the Tigers, a kicker losing his range was an oddly familiar occurrence. During their championship run last year they benefited from bad games by two of the Southeastern Conference's best--Billy Bennett and Jonathan Nichols--in wins over Georgia and Mississippi.

Another kicker looked like he would succumb to the Tigers' odd hex on Saturday, when Auburn's John Vaughn knocked a game-tying PAT attempt wide left with just over a minute left.

But LSU was apparently out of luck. A penalty gave Vaughn another attempt, which he made to give Auburn a 10-9 victory and the early lead in the SEC West.

LSU has had its own kicking issues. The Tigers found themselves a point short against Auburn because Ryan Gaudet missed a PAT. And Gaudet was only called on because starter Chris Jackson had already missed two extra points this season.

In the SEC East, Tennessee's James Wilhoit went from goat to hero against Florida. The first missed extra point of the sophomore's career left the Volunteers trailing 28-27 with less than four minutes left.

Like Vaughn, Wilhoit got a chance to redeem himself, but in far more dramatic fashion. Wilhoit nailed a game-winning 50-yard field with 6 seconds left.

"Just because I made the field goal doesn't make me more important than anybody else," Wilhoit said. "We played 60 minutes, and we all made plays. It just happened that mine was the final one."

Other kickers weren't as fortunate as Wilhoit and Vaughn.

Arizona's Nick Folk missed from 43 yards early in the game, then from 47 with less than a minute left and the Wildcats lost to Wisconsin 9-7.

San Diego State's upset bid at Michigan was foiled by two failed field goal attempts in the fourth quarter by Garrett Palmer. The Aztecs lost 24-21 and the Wolverines avoided a second straight loss that would have all but eliminated them from the national title hunt midway into September.

Michigan's rival Ohio State is still unbeaten thanks to the stellar kicking of Mike Nugent--and a miss by Marshall's Ian O'Connor two weeks ago.

The Buckeyes were in danger of being upset at home by Marshall in their second game, but O'Connor missed a 35-yard field goal with just over three minutes left that would have given the Thundering Herd the lead. Nugent then won the game with a 55-yarder as time expired.

He followed that up by tying a school record with five field goals in a 22-14 win over North Carolina State on Saturday.

"If you know us, you know our formula," Ohio State coach Jim Tressel said. "We tell our quarterbacks, 'When we get to a certain point, we've got the three. Don't foul up the three.'"

Auburn coach Tommy Tuberville doesn't see kickers getting worse, just a few high-profile mishaps.

"It's more than just the kicker. It starts with the snapper and holder, and everybody goes hand in hand. I don't think it's anything new," he said.

Ole Miss coach David Cutcliffe said all the close games and intense scrutiny might be taking a toll on kickers.

"I think it's probably tougher emotionally," said Cutcliffe, whose Rebels won their first game on Saturday with a field goal in overtime against Vanderbilt. "Plenty of close games come down to is that place-kicker going to hit. It used to be a game of inches, now it's a game of toes."

Still, many coaches are reluctant to use one of their precious 85 scholarships on kickers, leading to more walk-ons handling the important duties.

And if the NFL is any indication, it would appear that reliable kickers are getting harder to find. Gary Anderson and Morten Andersen, both over 40, are still on NFL rosters.

Unfortunately, neither has any college eligibility left.

Auburn stamps itself an SEC contender

JOHN ZENOR, September 19, 2004

All of a sudden, the expectations are soaring again for No. 9 Auburn.

The biggest difference is the Tigers earned the accolades on the field this time, with Saturday's gutsy 10-9 win over No. 13 LSU.

"We're 3-0, we beat the defending national champions _ I hope it's a momentum game," said Courtney Taylor, who caught the game-winning touchdown pass. "A lot of teams that face us now, that just puts a bigger target on us, just like they had a bigger target on them."

With the win, Auburn (3-0, 2-0 Southeastern

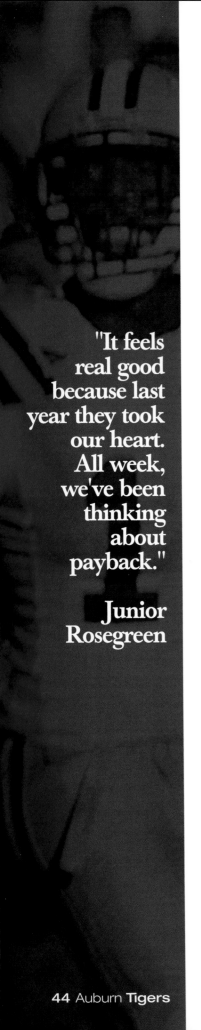

"It feels real good because last year they took our heart. All week, we've been thinking about payback."

Junior Rosegreen

Conference) became the early Western Division front-runner and moved into the top 10 for the first time since last year's embarrassing season-opening loss to Southern California.

The team displayed many of the qualities that were expected to land coach Tommy Tuberville's Tigers a league title last season: swarming defense, sturdy running game and offensive balance.

Tuberville stopped short of calling it a milestone victory for his team, describing it instead as "a good starting point for this season."

"We didn't play a perfect game by any stretch of the imagination, but we did play with a lot of desire," Tuberville said Sunday. "Is this a turning point? No, I think it's just a point that people will recognize that we've got a pretty decent team and things are going to just heat up on us.

"We're going to see if we can handle it."

Auburn dealt nicely with the pressure Saturday, persevering against a stingy defense until scraping together an arduous 12- play, 59-yard drive in the final minutes.

Jason Campbell hit Taylor on a 16-yarder with 1:14 left on a third-and-12 play for the win. Three plays earlier, they also paired up to convert on fourth-and-12.

"We kept pounding, we kept running the ball, we threw it, we made some plays," Tuberville said. "And finally we put enough together to win the game."

Defensive end Stanley McClover thinks any questions about Auburn's young defense were answered.

"We just felt like we had a lot to prove (Saturday), so we feel like there shouldn't be any more questions," McClover said.

Auburn kept putting LSU (2-1, 1-0) in bad field position, and quarterbacks JaMarcus Russell and Marcus Randall had little success digging the Tigers out.

Auburn also rebounded from LSU's fast start. Randall led LSU on a 14-play, 80-yard touchdown march to open the game, bringing back memories of his team's 21-0 first-quarter barrage in a blowout win last year.

Auburn showed resilience this time, allowing only a field goal the rest of the way and pitching a second-half shutout.

"We learned from that," said Bret Eddins, who had a key sack of Russell late in the third quarter. "If that hadn't happened, I don't know what the outcome would have been."

LSU coach Nick Saban continued to platoon quarterbacks, but neither stood out.

"I don't think it threw off the rhythm," Randall said of the quarterback rotation. "There were a lot of mental errors that took place."

LSU won a national championship with one loss last season, so the Tigers know there's plenty of season left for a recovery.

"We didn't approach the game like a season-ending game," Saban said. "Like I told our players, this is a learning experience."

	LSU	Auburn
First Downs	18	16
3rd-Down Efficiency	6-15-40%	4-13-31%
4th-Down Efficiency	0-0--%	1-2-50%
Total net yards	308	301
Net yards rushing	140	131
Net yards passing	168	170
Penalties-yards	6-37	5-60
Time of Possession	30:20	29:40

Auburn's Stanley McClover picks up coach Tommy Tuberville after their 10-9 win against LSU.

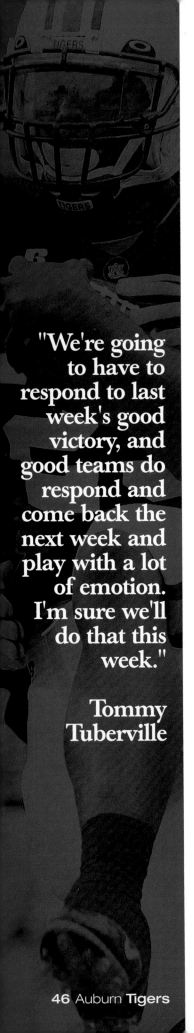

"We're going to have to respond to last week's good victory, and good teams do respond and come back the next week and play with a lot of emotion. I'm sure we'll do that this week."

Tommy Tuberville

No. 9 Auburn 33, The Citadel 3

September 25, 2004

Tigers try not to overlook The Citadel

JOHN ZENOR, September 24, 2004

If ever Auburn was susceptible to the temptation of taking it easy against a weak opponent, this might be the time. The ninth-ranked Tigers (3-0) host The Citadel (0-1) on Saturday, a sandwich game that certainly won't have the luster of facing LSU last week or Tennessee next week.

Auburn coach Tommy Tuberville figures his team's ability to come back down from the euphoria of a win over the defending co-national champs will say a lot about the Tigers.

"We're going to have to respond to last week's good victory, and good teams do respond and come back the next week and play with a lot of emotion," Tuberville said. "I'm sure we'll do that this week."

The Citadel has only played one game after postponing its opener against Charleston Southern because of Hurricane Frances.

The Bulldogs are 10-70-4 against Southeastern Conference teams, with their last win coming against Arkansas in 1992.

Still, first-year coach John Zernhelt said his approach doesn't change just because his team is playing a high-profile opponent.

"We try to treat every opponent as if they are Auburn," Zernhelt said. "That's the approach we take to every game. We treat everybody like they were Auburn or Alabama or Clemson or whoever it is."

Tuberville is seeking a similar approach for his players _ treating The Citadel the same as every other opponent.

"The coaches do a good job of instilling in us that we have to work on ourselves as a team and get better each and every week," Auburn tailback Ronnie Brown said. "We have the potential to do some great things at the end of the season.

"When it comes to games like this, we don't really worry too much about the opponent. We worry about ourselves and try to correct some of the mistakes we made the previous week."

The Tigers certainly have plenty to play for now, after vaulting into the top 10. They have won five straight games dating back to last season and could stretch the streak to six for the first time since opening 6-0 in 1997.

However, Tennessee looms, making it even harder for the Tigers to keep their minds on The Citadel.

"It's hard, but you've just got to instill that you take it one game at a time, or a team

The Citadel's Nehemiah Hawkins looks for daylight against Auburn during the first quarter.

Auburn **Tigers**

(left) Auburn's Carnell Williams scores in the second quarter against The Citadel. (above) The Citadel's Joshua Lawson knocks the ball away from Auburn's Carnell Williams (24) during the second quarter.

like that can come in and beat you," cornerback Carlos Rogers said.

The Citadel's biggest challenge will be solving Auburn's defense, allowing just over a touchdown a game. The Bulldogs managed just 137 yards against Appalachian State, a I-AA power.

They are led by running back Nehemiah Broughton, who accounted for 92 of those yards in rushing and receiving.

"We can't lose focus, and we can't lose sight of our goals," Auburn safety Junior Rosegreen said. "As long as we keep sight of our goals, we'll be all right."

No. 9 Auburn 33,
The Citadel 3

JOHN ZENOR, September 25, 2004

Undefeated Auburn got just what it needed in its sandwich game between a couple of high-stakes contests.

The ninth-ranked Tigers got plenty of rest for their starters, solid games from Carnell Williams and Jason

Campbell and production from the backups in a stress-free 33-3 win over Division I-AA's The Citadel on Saturday.

"We took care of business," Auburn coach Tommy Tuberville said. "It wasn't anything exciting. It was just one of those days when we went out and got it done.

"I could tell the focus was on a little bit different team than the one we were playing today."

Such as, perhaps, No. 11 Tennessee, next week's opponent on the road? Or even No. 13 LSU, which the Tigers squeaked by a week ago?

Campbell was 11-of-14 for 194 yards and Williams rushed for 95 yards and a 1-yard touchdown on 22 carries, then both players sat out the second half.

The Tigers (4-0) had no problem overcoming a few sloppy plays against the Bulldogs (0-2) in a workmanlike tuneup for next week's showdown against the Volunteers.

Williams admitted Tennessee was "kind of in the back of my mind."

"I'm not saying we overlooked The Citadel, but in the back of our minds we were kind of thinking about Tennessee," said Williams, who lost two first-half fumbles in Bulldogs territory.

The Tigers have a six-game winning streak for the first time since opening the 1997 season 6-0, and only missed their second shutout of the season on a field goal in the fourth quarter.

"After a big win like last week, sometimes it can be tough to come out and get focused for the game," said safety Will Herring, who had an interception on The Citadel's first play. "We just wanted to go out and get better because we know we have to play our best game next week in Knoxville."

Auburn outgained The Citadel 593-169 in yards overall, allowing just 71 yards passing and eight first downs. Most fans left by the fourth quarter.

The Tigers led 23-0 at the half despite a handful of mistakes, and the backups didn't let up much. Only LSU has scored on Auburn in the first half this season.

Backup Ronnie Brown, the league's No. 4 rusher, sat out the game with a sore hamstring. Redshirt freshman Carl Stewart gained 91 yards on 10 carries in his place, including a 1-yard TD.

Campbell scored on a 1-yard sneak. Backup Brandon Cox came in late in the first half and went 11-of-17 for 165 yards, including a 10-yard TD pass to Jamoga Ramsey.

The Citadel's only points came on a 28-yard field goal with 6:01 left by Blake Vandiver, set up by Ern Hill's 79-yard kickoff return from his own end zone.

"They really worked hard to do what they are coached to do, and I am proud of them," Bulldogs coach John Zerhelt said. "I thought that they never quit, and they played hard."

The Bulldogs' starting quarterback, Justin Hardin, finished 3-of- 8 for 16 yards. Backup Duran Lawson was 3-of-6 for 55 yards, most on a 42-yarder to Gary Domanski.

Tailback Nehemiah Broughton said the Bulldogs weren't intimidated.

"We didn't feel like underdogs today," said Broughton, who had 73 yards on 19 carries. "We never feel over-matched."

	Citadel	Auburn
First Downs	8	33
3rd-Down Efficiency	3-13-23%	7-11-64%
4th-Down Efficiency	0-0--%	0-0--%
Total net yards	169	593
Net yards rushing	98	234
Net yards passing	71	359
Penalties-yards	5-50	6-61
Time of Possession	25:53	34:7

Auburn quarterback Jason Campbell throws under presure from The Citadel's Brandon Hawkins and Michael Ballentine during the Tigers' 33-8 victory.

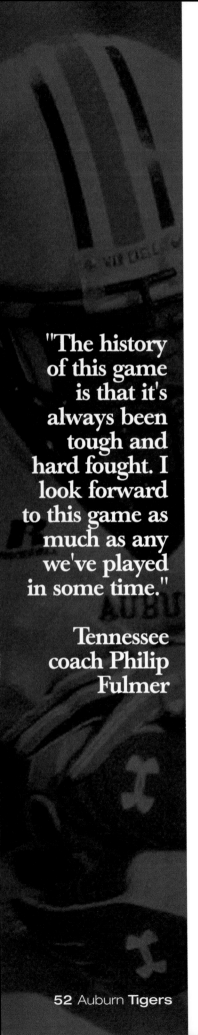

"The history
of this game
is that it's
always been
tough and
hard fought. I
look forward
to this game as
much as any
we've played
in some time."

Tennessee
coach Philip
Fulmer

No. 8 Auburn 34, No. 10 Tennessee 10

October 2, 2004

Auburn, Tennessee put rushing to the test

ELIZABETH A. DAVIS, September 30, 2004

It's Auburn vs. Tennessee—let the tailbacks loose. The eighth-ranked Tigers' 1-2 punch of Carnell "Cadillac" Williams and Ronnie Brown hope to repeat the performance they had last year against Tennessee.

The No. 10 Volunteers say their running game has improved from last season behind Cedric Houston and Gerald Riggs, and they're ready to put it to the test Saturday night when they host Auburn (4- 0, 2-0 Southeastern Conference).

"(Tennessee coach Phillip) Fulmer has always wanted to run the football. They have been searching for the running game and found it," Auburn coach Tommy Tuberville said. "It's just a matter of saying we are going to be a better running football team and being successful."

Tennessee (3-0, 1-0) leads the SEC in rushing at 263.3 yards an average per game, and Auburn is fourth at 210.5 yards.

Houston is third among the SEC's top 10 rushers followed by Williams and Brown, and Riggs, is seventh.

And to think they could have all been on the same team.

Williams verbally committed to Tennessee before Tuberville made a big push to change his mind, and Brown considered the Vols too.

Add Tennessee's Jabari Davis with Houston and Williams, and that would have made three Parade All-Americans in the 2001 freshman class.

Williams and Brown showed the Vols what they were missing in Auburn's 28-21 win last year. The Tigers pounded Tennessee for 264 yards on the ground, the most rushing yards the Vols' defense gave up last year.

Williams had 185 yards, while Brown added 65 more. They scored a touchdown apiece.

"Just going up to the week of the game, there was a lot of talk about the running back situation of both teams," Brown said about last year. "It was exciting when we got in the game, both Carnell and myself being able to stay loose and not get too tired."

Good news for the rest of the SEC is that both Williams and Brown are seniors.

"Those two running backs have dealt out a lot of misery in this conference for the year they've been there," Fulmer said.

Tennessee's tailbacks hardly had a chance to show what they could do at Auburn a

Auburn's Jason Campbell (17) looks down field for a receiver during the first quarter.

Auburn's Ben Obomanu (2) catches a pass for a touchdown as Tennessee's Johnathan Hefney (33) tries to rip the ball loose during the first quarter.

year ago. The Vols trailed 14-0 in the first quarter and opted to go with a hurry-up offense using almost all passing. Tennessee finished the game with 4 yards rushing.

In the first three games so far this season, the tailbacks and offensive line have showed a huge improvement.

"The running game has pretty much been the kick starter for the offense in every game we've played. We've pretty much forced the running game on everybody and made them respect it," Riggs said.

Tennessee's improved rushing has helped take some pressure off its freshmen quarterbacks. The Vols have decided to start Erik Ainge against Auburn instead of Brent Schaeffer, who was the starter for the first three games.

But both teams will count on their quarterbacks to make some plays to keep the defenses busy.

Auburn QB Jason Campbell led a 12-play, 59-yard drive capped by his 16-yard touchdown pass to Courtney Taylor with 1:14 left to give Auburn a 10-9 win over LSU two weeks ago.

"Their quarterback and their passing game are much improved," Fulmer said of Auburn. "And that makes them a much bigger threat to manage."

Auburn vs. Tennessee: a rivalry reborn with high rankings

ELIZABETH A. DAVIS, October 1, 2004

Auburn vs. Tennessee was always a high point on the schedule. Then the Southeastern Conference split into divisions in 1992, and the teams stopped playing every year.

Saturday night's matchup, however, is a bit like the old days and could go a long way toward determining who plays for the league championship.

"The history of this game, having been part of it as a player, an assistant coach and now as head coach, is that it's always been tough and hard fought," Tennessee coach Phillip Fulmer said. "I look forward to this game as much as any we've played in some time."

No. 8 Auburn (4-0, 2-0) and No. 10 Tennessee (3-0, 1-0) are two of the three remaining undefeated teams in the league. Georgia is the other.

They haven't met as top-10 teams since 1990, a game that ended in a tie. The Tigers have not won in Knoxville since 1983, a stretch of three losses and the tie.

The slide started when Tennessee stunned then-No. 1

Auburn and Heisman Trophy winner Bo Jackson 38-20 in 1985. The Vols went on to win the SEC championship that year.

Now the Tigers are bringing a different star running back to Neyland Stadium. Carnell "Cadillac" Williams forms a 1-2 punch with his backup Ronnie Brown, and they have high hopes for their final year at Auburn.

"The world is going to be watching two undefeated teams, two top- 10 teams. Whoever wins this game, the sky's the limit," Williams said.

Tennessee's tailbacks are looking to show the Vols' power running game is back. Cedric Houston and Gerald Riggs lead the SEC's top rushing offense.

Auburn's tailbacks ran all over Tennessee last year in a 28-20 victory on The Plains. The Vols had 4 yards rushing to 264 for Auburn.

"The memory of being down there last year was not a whole lot of fun," Fulmer said.

The biggest change from last year's game is Tennessee's two- quarterback system. Casey Clausen had been a four-year starter. Erik Ainge will start in place of fellow freshman Brent Schaeffer, but Fulmer said both will play.

The Vols attribute part of the offense's success to a tougher offensive live, better running by the tailbacks and a slew of big- play receivers.

"I think we have the best receiving corps—one through eight—in the country," Ainge said. "They haven't faced a team like us yet."

Auburn's defense is rugged. The Tigers held LSU to nine points, and their scoring defense ranks No. 1 in the SEC and second in the nation at 6.5 points a game.

Tennessee's secondary lost three starters from a year ago. Statistically, the Vols have the worst pass defense in the conference.

But Auburn quarterback Jason Campbell must contend with the din of a stadium that rocks. Tennessee set an attendance record of 109,061 at the Florida game two weeks ago.

"You come to college for big games like this," Campbell said. "It's just a matter of us communicating with each other. ... As long as we're communicating and getting our assignments, we should be OK."

Tennessee had beaten Auburn four games in a row until last year's loss. One of those victories was in the 1997 SEC championship game, and the Vols also won in 1998, the year they won the national championship, and 1999.

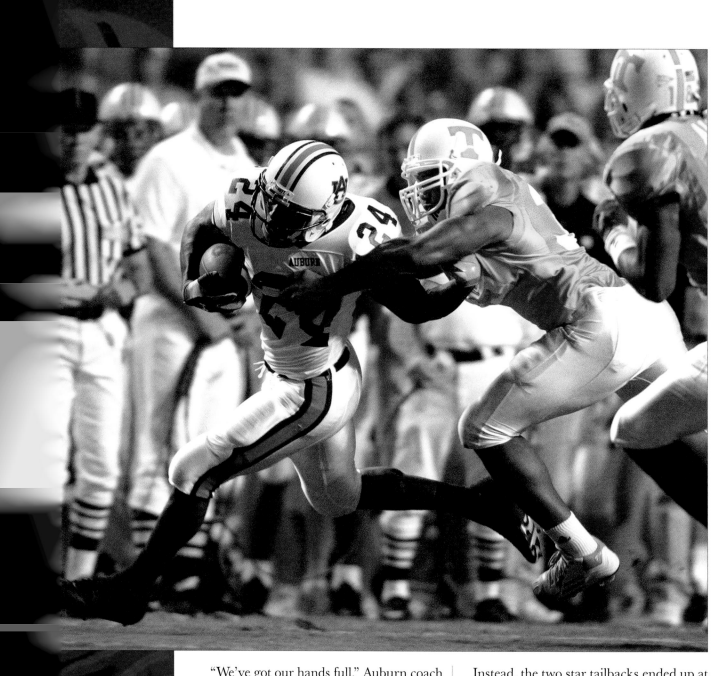

"We've got our hands full," Auburn coach Tommy Tuberville said. "This will be a high-profile game for our players to show how much better they have gotten."

Auburn tailbacks nearly landed with Vols

JOHN ZENOR, September 28, 2004

For both Carnell Williams and Ronnie Brown, the first choice was to play for Tennessee.

Instead, the two star tailbacks ended up at Auburn and will be playing at Neyland Stadium for the first time Saturday, when the eighth-ranked Tigers visit the No. 10 Volunteers.

"Man, I can't really explain the feeling I've got right now, just going back there and playing ball," Williams said. "I've sat in those stands.

"At one time, that's where I thought I was going."

Then, coach Tommy Tuberville and six

(above) Williams had 24 carries for 98 yards as Auburn defeated Tennessee 34-10. (right) Auburn's Junior Rosegreen, right, grabs an interception as Tennessee receiver Robert Meachem (3) pursues in the second quarter.

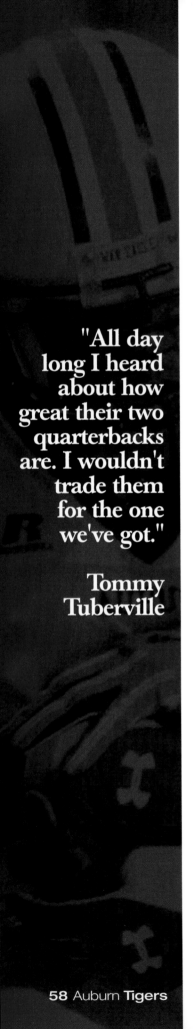

"All day long I heard about how great their two quarterbacks are. I wouldn't trade them for the one we've got."

Tommy Tuberville

assistants visited his house in Attalla, Ala., and persuaded Williams not to cancel his visit to Auburn.

Brown, from Cartersville, Ga., also verbally committed to Tennessee, but changed his plans partly because of a recruiting scandal at the time that he thought might land the Vols on NCAA probation.

"I just changed my mind a couple of days before signing day," he said.

Good thing for Auburn, too.

Williams and Brown, who arrived a year apart, have become two of the school's most prolific runners. They rank fourth and fifth in the league in rushing even though Brown sat out The Citadel game to rest a tender hamstring.

Both were big parts of Auburn's win over the Vols (3-0, 1-0) last season. Williams had 36 carries for 185 yards while Brown gained 65 yards on 12 carries, and both scored touchdowns for the Tigers (4- 0, 2-0 Southeastern Conference).

"That game was the first time we really showed the 1-2 punch with Ronnie and Carnell," said Tuberville. "I mean, one guy got tired and the other one went in and we never missed a beat. The other times one was playing because the other was injured.

"I thought that was really the coming-out party of both those guys having a big game on each side."

Williams and Brown share the backfield at times in Auburn's new offense, and both have lined up at receiver.

Williams' senior season hasn't gone quite as well as expected. He has 395 yards and three touchdowns, but has been held shy of 100 yards in the past two games with defenses keying on him. He doesn't have a run longer than 22 yards.

Quarterback Jason Campbell has a simple explanation for that.

"Every time he gets the ball, there's four of five guys trying to tackle him," Campbell said. "They're trying to swarm to him."

Brown is averaging 8.7 yards on 31 carries, including a 59- yarder against Mississippi State when both reached 100 yards for the first time in the same game.

Tennessee coach Phillip Fulmer isn't fretting too much over losing out on Brown and Williams. He has Cedric Houston and Gerald Riggs powering the SEC's top running game.

"Carnell has had a heck of a career there, and Ced has had a good career here and he's having a great year so far this year," Fulmer said.

Williams went to a couple of games at Neyland Stadium while in high school.

"After my visit with them, I really felt like that's where I was going, because I felt at home," he said. "Coach Tubs came to my home and changed my mind."

Tuberville targeted Williams shortly after arriving at Auburn in 1998. The first prep game he attended was when Williams and Etowah County won the Alabama state championship.

"You could tell the difference, what type of running back he was," Tuberville said. "He set himself apart from everybody on the field. We knew how good he was, and he hasn't disappointed. He's been even better than we thought."

No. 8 Auburn 34, No. 10 Tennessee 10

RALPH D. RUSSO, October 3, 2004

Jason Campbell is running the West Coast offense like an old pro and turning Auburn into a national title contender in the process.

The often-criticized quarterback threw for 252 yards and two touchdowns, and the eighth-ranked Tigers overwhelmed No. 10 Tennessee 34-10 on Saturday night.

Carnell Williams and Ronnie Brown each ran for a touchdown to complement Campbell, and the Tigers' swarming defense made Tennessee's two freshmen quarterbacks look like neophytes for the first time this season. Junior Rosegreen had four interceptions to set a record for

Auburn (5-0, 3-0 Southeastern Conference) and tie the SEC mark.

"All day long I heard about how great their two quarterbacks are," Auburn coach Tommy Tuberville said. "I wouldn't trade them for the one we've got. (Campbell) played a great football game."

Erik Ainge got his first start for the Volunteers (3-1, 1-1) after racking up the best passer rating in the SEC over the first three games. The promotion did no good. He went 17-for-35 for 173 yards with four interceptions and a fumble.

Fellow freshman Brent Schaeffer had little success in his first game as a reliever. He also threw an interception and went 1-for-5.

"They're freshmen, they're going to learn," Vols coach Phillip Fulmer said. "We played against a better football team tonight."

Campbell has often received the blame from fans and media for Auburn's past offensive inconsistency, despite playing for four offensive coordinators in four seasons.

"That is something I have never worried about in my career," Campbell said. "I always knew I wasn't getting the credit people should give me, but that's one thing I didn't worry about."

He is finally flourishing under coordinator Al Borges' West Coast offense, with its multiple shifts, quick throws and moving pockets. He also is showing the confidence and poise of a quarterback with 32 career starts.

Campbell summed up the transformation simply, "They're giving me the opportunity to use all my abilities."

Against the Vols, he looked off defenders and stepped up in the pocket. He threw with fine touch over defenders and zipped passes in between them. Campbell was 12-for-15 in the first half for 240 yards to lead the Tigers to a 31-3 lead.

The Tigers took the field knowing that their two main SEC West rivals–LSU and Arkansas–had lost. As if bolstered by the opportunity to grab command of the division, Auburn controlled the first quarter.

The Tigers forced a three-and-out on the first series of the game, got a piece of Tennessee's punt, and Campbell and his two star tailbacks went to work at their own 45.

The Tigers drove the field with a mix of power running and quick passes. Brown finished the job by bowling over Tennessee's Jason Allen, knocking the safety's helmet off on the way to a 9-yard touchdown run.

After the Vols responded with a field goal, the Tigers marched down field again but couldn't complete the drive this time. Brown fumbled at the 5 and Tennessee recovered at the 1.

It was only a temporary reprieve for the Vols.

Ainge lost the ball on a sneak and Auburn was back in the red zone. Campbell then made it 14-3 with a 5-yard pass to Ben Obomanu.

When Williams ran over Allen for a 5-yard touchdown in the second quarter it was 24-3 and most of the 107,828 fans at Neyland Stadium were stunned silent.

"We had so many mistakes we put them in perfect position to win," Tennessee linebacker Kevin Burnett said. "Mental errors, missed tackles. That comes back to hurt you in the end."

Just when it looked as though Tennessee might make a game of it, Auburn's defense came up with its third takeaway. Travis Williams picked off Ainge's tipped pass at the LSU 32 with 2:05 left in the half.

Auburn wasn't about to get conservative.

Campbell went deep on the next play, hitting Brown for 38 yards. Moments later, Campbell threw a bullet to Courtney Taylor slanting over the middle and the receiver broke free for a 31-yard TD play and a 28-point halftime lead.

Rosegreen picked off three passes in a second half that was otherwise a formality.

For Tennessee, it gets no easier next week; the Vols go to Georgia, which made a statement of its own with a 45-16 victory over LSU on Saturday.

"We have a lot left to go," Vols tackle Michael Munoz said. "We still control our destiny in the SEC East."

Auburn, a team that fell far short of lofty expectations last season, now has a 1 1/2-game lead in the SEC West and its first win at Knoxville since 1983.

"We had something to prove," Tuberville said. "We got better each snap. We got stronger each snap."

No. 6 Auburn takes control of SEC West

ELIZABETH A. DAVIS, October 3, 2004

Five games into the season, Auburn has established itself as the clear favorite in the SEC West–and a serious contender in the national championship race.

With a dominating 34-10 win at Tennessee on Saturday night, the sixth-ranked Tigers (5-0, 3-0) seem well on their way to going to the conference championship game for the first time since 2000.

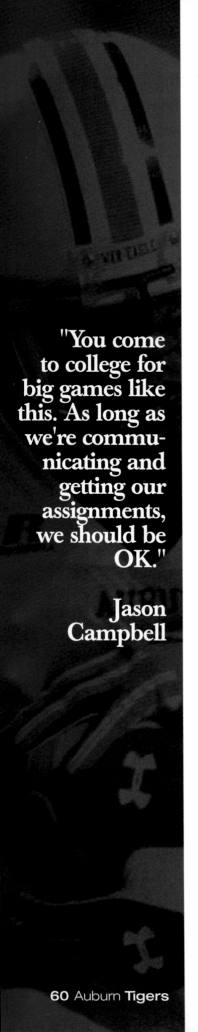

"You come to college for big games like this. As long as we're communicating and getting our assignments, we should be OK."

Jason Campbell

The Tigers haven't won a title game since the league split into divisions in 1992.

"It just makes the next conference game just that much more important," Auburn coach Tommy Tuberville said. "We're not going to start talking about anything other than playing the next game. Obviously there will be a lot of talk about it. But we've got a good start—a lot better than we did last year."

Auburn lost its first two games last season before winning five straight, including a victory over Tennessee. The Tigers then fell to LSU, Mississippi and Georgia and finished third in the West.

Auburn has already beaten No. 24 LSU this season, leaving Georgia as the only remaining undefeated conference opponent on its schedule. The Tigers host the third-ranked Bulldogs on Nov. 13.

For the Volunteers (3-1, 1-1) a second straight loss to Auburn was a sobering reminder that winning the East will be a formidable task. Tennessee, which fell seven spots in the AP poll to No. 17, goes to Georgia next week.

"I'm very disappointed in our team, but we have to go to Georgia and win anyway quite likely to win the East," Tennessee coach Phillip Fulmer said.

The Tigers offense proved to be too much for Tennessee. Carnell Williams and Ronnie Brown bulldozed over defenders to each score a touchdown, and Brown led Auburn in receiving with 79 yards on six catches.

A key for the Tigers was quarterback Jason Campbell, who threw for 252 yards and two touchdowns. He led Auburn to a 31-3 lead at halftime, effectively ending the game.

And the Auburn defense showed why it holds opponents to a paltry 6.5 points a contest. Junior Rosegreen tied an SEC record with four interceptions and Travis

Williams also picked off a pass.

Tennessee started Erik Ainge at quarterback for the first time, but neither he nor fellow freshman Brent Schaeffer could get Tennessee's offense rolling. Ainge, who was the league's most efficient passer before the game, was intercepted four times and fumbled once.

The Vols looked discombobulated from the start.

Tennessee called a timeout on their second play from scrimmage and then appeared to have trouble at the line before Ainge threw an incomplete pass.

Even All-American punter Dustin Colquitt had an off night, averaging 35 yards on two punts, nine yards off his conference- leading average.

"I take full responsibility. I didn't do enough to get the team ready," Fulmer said. "We have good leadership and there was still energy after the game. No one was ducking their head.

"We have to pick ourselves off the turf and go play again."

	Auburn	Tennessee
First Downs	17	22
3rd-Down Efficiency	6-13-46%	5-12-42%
4th-Down Efficiency	0-1-0%	1-1-100%
Total net yards	400	293
Net yards rushing	148	107
Net yards passing	252	186
Penalties-yards	9-71	5-41
Time of Possession	36:6	23:54

Tennessee's C.J. Fayton is tackled by Auburn's Montavis Pitts during the first quarter.

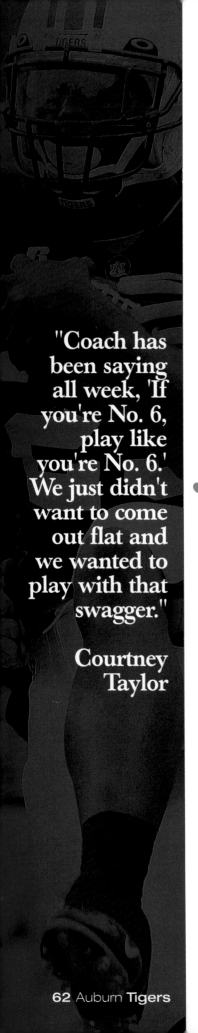

"Coach has
been saying
all week, 'If
you're No. 6,
play like
you're No. 6.'
We just didn't
want to come
out flat and
we wanted to
play with that
swagger."

Courtney
Taylor

No. 6 Auburn 52, Louisiana Tech 7

October 9, 2004

Auburn DB specializing in picks, trash-talking

JOHN ZENOR, October 6, 2004

Junior Rosegreen likes to make an impression. Consider Auburn coach Tommy Tuberville's first glimpse of him on a recruiting trip.

"He came out to my school and he saw me out there just talking trash, knocking folks out," said the Tigers' chatty safety. "Then he came up to me and was like, 'Son, you talk a lot of trash but you back it up.'"

Rosegreen still talks a lot, but boy is he backing it up for No. 6 Auburn.

After telling teammates he'd get three interceptions against Tennessee, the senior did one better. He tied the Southeastern Conference's 65-year-old record with four picks in a 34-10 victory Saturday, matching the mark set by John Nix of Mississippi State against Arkansas in 1939.

Only two other Division I-A players have as many as four interceptions all season: Marshall's Chris Royal (five) and New Mexico's Brandon Payne (four).

Two weeks earlier, Rosegreen ended LSU's rally hopes with an interception in the final moments of that 10-9 victory.

Talk away, Junior.

"Really, I don't look at that as anything big," Rosegreen said. "I'm supposed to do things like that. I'm supposed to make big things happen."

Rosegreen has been a cornerstone of Auburn's defense for four years, a three-year starter known for his gift of gab as much as his athletic abilities.

"Junior's not at a loss for words, ever," Tuberville said. "He's got a lot of confidence in himself, which is good."

Rosegreen is hoping college football fans around the country know his name after the Tennessee game.

"If they don't know, I'm going to continue to come out and make big plays," said Rosegreen, who had only three career interceptions coming into the season. "Eventually they'll know who I am."

He appears to come by his confidence naturally. He said his father, Norman, told him before both the LSU and Tennessee games he would come up with big interceptions.

"Whatever my daddy says," Rosegreen said, "looks like it's going to happen."

And his teammates? Well, what do they know? Several were teasing him after the third interception against the Volunteers, telling him he wouldn't get another one.

Louisiana Tech quarterback Matt Kubik is sacked by Auburn's Quentin Groves.

Rosegreen isn't all talk, even though he's awfully good at it. The past two years, Auburn coaches have given him the team's offseason conditioning award.

Defensive tackle Tommy Jackson likes Rosegreen because he's reliable on the field ("Junior's going to get the job done") and off it.

"He's a big brother," Jackson said. "If I need a ride or something, I'll call Junior. He's one of those kind of dudes. What happened (Saturday) night couldn't have happened to a greater guy. He's a great guy, really."

Tuberville calls Rosegreen a comedian.

But don't let the cocky demeanor fool you.

"The players like him because they know everything he does is for the betterment of the team," Tuberville said. "He's a true team player."

No. 6 Auburn 52, La. Tech 7

JOHN ZENOR, October 9, 2004

Letdown? No chance for No. 6 Auburn, which rolled past Louisiana Tech 52-7 Saturday in a game the Tigers could easily have overlooked.

Instead, they got another easy victory and almost certainly a chance to continue their rapid ascent in the national rankings with losses by No. 5 Texas and No. 3 Georgia.

Still, coach Tommy Tuberville's focus was on, well, his team's focus.

"That's good to read and talk about, but it doesn't make any difference," Tuberville said. "If you're up there one week, you don't get a trophy for that."

They do get to enjoy their front-runner

> "The atmosphere is crazy around here. I wouldn't trade it."
>
> Carnell Williams

"I was like, 'They've got to try and throw it so I'm going to try to be in the right spot at the right time,'" Rosegreen said.

And? "I was in the right spot at the right time."

For all his outspoken ways, Rosegreen follows a trash-talking etiquette. He seldom badmouths an opponent (before the game, at least) and takes a businesslike approach to the art of talking smack.

"You've just got to be smart," Rosegreen said. "A lot of these young people today they get caught up in the hype and they're so hyped they want to talk trash.

"You can't talk trash in the papers because that's nothing but bulletin board (material). That's giving the other team the upper hand."

(above) Louisiana Tech's Lee Johnson, left, and Robert Burrell, right, stop Auburn running back Carl Stewart in the fourth quarter. (right) Louisiana Tech running back Ryan Moats is thrown down by Auburn's Anthony Campbell, bottom, and Doug Langenfeld, left. Moats, the nation's 2nd leading rusher, sprained his ankle on the play and did not return to action.

Auburn's Ronnie Brown scores on a three-yard run in the first quarter as Louisiana Tech's Corey Brazil and Lee Johnson defend.

status as the lone remaining unbeaten in the Southeastern Conference, fresh from a 34-10 victory at Tennessee, which beat Georgia 19-14. Oklahoma topped Texas 12-0.

Next up for Auburn, 6-0 for the first time since 1997, is Western Division rival Arkansas.

Jason Campbell passed for 201 yards and two touchdowns, including a school-record 87-yarder to Silas Daniels. Ronnie Brown ran for 109 yards on 10 carries and Carlos Rogers returned an interception 53 yards for a touchdown.

"Coach has been saying all week, 'If you're No. 6, play like you're No. 6,'" receiver Courtney Taylor said. "We just didn't want to come out flat and we wanted to play with that swagger."

The Tigers, who have risen from preseason No. 17, have had only one game decided by under 24 points and allowed one touchdown or fewer in all but one game. Louisiana Tech (3-3) was impressed after a four-week stretch that included losses to Miami and Tennessee and a win over Fresno State.

"Auburn is a very complete team right now," Bulldogs coach Jack Bicknell said. "They've got great wide receivers, a great quarterback, great running backs and a great defense.

"They're probably one of the best teams in the country."

One of the best tailbacks didn't get much chance to shine. Louisiana Tech's Ryan Moats, the nation's No. 2 rusher, limped off the field in the first quarter with a sprained right ankle and didn't return.

"My ankle is OK," said Moats, who had no yards on three carries after averaging 185.6 per game coming in. "The doctors did not want to chance (further) injury."

The Tigers still haven't given up a rushing touchdown and collected nine sacks, forcing three turnovers.

Carnell Williams had 56 yards on 12 carries and also scored while setting up a TD with a 50-yard punt return. He wasn't fretting over his modest rushing numbers.

"The atmosphere is crazy around here," Williams said. "I wouldn't trade it."

Coming off a career game against Tennessee, Campbell supplied a characteristically efficient 13-of-18 passing performance.

The teams exchanged a flurry of big plays midway through the third quarter, mostly courtesy of Auburn.

The Tigers capped an 11-play, 99-yard drive with Campbell's 9-yard touchdown pass to Ben Obomanu midway through the third quarter. Tramon Williams nearly made a leaping interception but was bobbling the ball as he fell backward in the end zone and Obomanu scooped it out of the air.

Brown had a tackle-breaking 43-yard run to set up the TD.

The Bulldogs answered on the next play with Matt Kubik's 78-yard scoring pass to Jonathan Holland, who had slipped behind safety Will Herring down the right sideline.

Three plays later, Campbell rolled right and hit a streaking Daniels, topping Auburn's record of 85 yards, accomplished twice before.

Two minutes later, Obomanu outfought Williams again for a 37-yard score from backup quarterback Brandon Cox. Cox attempted three passes, two for touchdowns.

Moats' sub, Freddie Franklin, gained 75 yards on 13 carries after coming in with zero yards on five carries.

Auburn outgained Louisiana Tech 472-222. The Bulldogs pushed into Auburn territory five times in the first half, but couldn't get points against the nation's No. 4 scoring defense and trailed 24-0.

The Tigers broke Alabama's 17-year-old SEC record of 199 consecutive successful extra points after their first TD.

	Louisiana Tech	Auburn
First Downs	12	18
3rd-Down Efficiency	2-14-14%	6-11-55%
4th-Down Efficiency	1-2-50%	0-2-0%
Total net yards	222	472
Net yards rushing	37	198
Net yards passing	185	274
Penalties-yards	7-58	8-73
Time of Possession	30:43	29:17

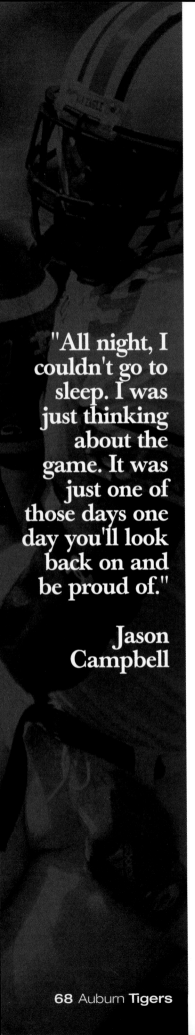

"All night, I couldn't go to sleep. I was just thinking about the game. It was just one of those days one day you'll look back on and be proud of."

Jason
Campbell

No. 4 Auburn 38, Arkansas 20

October 16, 2004

Auburn's undersized linebackers leading way

JOHN ZENOR, October 13, 2004

Travis Williams and Antarrious Williams don't look like the prototypical linebackers of Auburn's past.

Like last year, for instance.

Yet the speedy but undersized linebackers are producing big results in a defense that closely resembles last year's group only in production.

"You say they're small but they play like they're 6-4," coach Tommy Tuberville said. "They take linemen on. It's not like they're just run-around guys. They're very physical and strong. It's the added dimension of speed on your team. This entire defense is faster."

Travis Williams wants it clear: they may run like defensive backs but they hit like linebackers.

"We've got the speed and quickness of safeties, so that's a plus," he said. "But when we're in the box we're linebackers."

The Tigers' defense was loaded with questions before the season. Now, it appears they're just loaded, ranking fourth nationally in scoring defense and seventh

overall.

No. 4 Auburn (6-0, 3-0 Southeastern Conference) hasn't allowed a rushing touchdown and is actually giving up 25 fewer yards and five fewer points per game than last year's defense at this point.

That group was led by bigger, taller linebackers Dontarrious Thomas and Karlos Dansby, both all-SEC performers and second-round NFL draft picks. Three of the starting linemen also departed.

Travis Williams, a 6-foot-1, 209-pounder, leads the Tigers with 36 tackles and has five stops for a loss and two interceptions. Antarrious (no relation) is a 5-11, 208-pounder with 23 tackles, including a team-high six behind the line.

Linebackers coach Joe Whitt said he doesn't consider either player undersized.

"Otherwise we wouldn't have recruited them," Whitt said. "We thought they were big enough to play, good enough to play and would play and be successful."

Their speed and dependable tackling should be factors Saturday when Arkansas (3-2, 1-1) visits, led by fast and versatile quarterback Matt Jones.

Travis started all 12 games last season but was overshadowed by Dansby and Thomas despite finishing with 67 tackles. Antarrious has nearly reached his com-

---

Auburn quarterback Jason Campbell is tackled behind the line of scrimmage by Arkansas defender Jeremy Harrell and others during the second quarter.

(left) Arkansas receiver Marcus Monk drags along Auburn defender Karibi Dede after making a first-down catch and run in the second quarter. (above) Auburn's Jason Campbell pprepares to fire the ball as Arkansas's Pierre Brown bears down.

bined total of 27 tackles the past two years.

The other starter, Kevin Sears, is the more standard size at 6- 4, 236. He has 13 tackles, one fewer than his total as a freshman.

"We're playing seven defensive backs, that's what we're doing," Tuberville said. "We've got defensive backs bigger than our linebackers."

Cornerback Carlos Rogers is about the same size as the Williamses, but marvels at their ability to take on bigger running backs and linemen.

"I'm really impressed with them," the 6-1, 200-pound Rogers said. "I tell Travis all the time, 'I really love you two guys.' They're strong, they know the game. They're coming on, getting better and better each game."

Auburn remembers battering in Razorbacks' last visit

JOHN ZENOR, October 14, 2004

It was the ultimate insult for a hard-nosed defensive coach, Arkansas battering the Auburn defense like it had seldom been battered.

The final tally, 426 rushing yards and a 38-17 Arkansas victory, was largely the work of Fred Talley, a mostly unheralded runner whose 241 yards was the most ever allowed by the Tigers.

"They humiliated us, took our manhood, pride and all that," said Joe Whitt, Auburn's longtime linebackers coach. "I had never been around that. That was a first and hopefully a last."

A repeat of that 2002 performance seems highly unlikely when the Razorbacks (3-2, 1-1 Southeastern Conference) return to Jordan-Hare Stadium Saturday for a showdown with the fourth-ranked Tigers (6-0, 3-0).

Arkansas is a 13-point underdog, but last year's 10-3 upset loss to Auburn aside, the Razorbacks typically rise to the occasion against the Tigers.

They had won three of four meetings before last year's game. Auburn coach Tommy Tuberville, an Arkansas native, saw his home state team whip the Tigers by 25 and 24 points during that stretch, both times when Auburn was ranked and the Razorbacks weren't.

"They always play us tough, no matter what they're ranked or what we're ranked," Auburn tailback Carnell Williams said.

Clearly this is a different Auburn defense from the group Arkansas clobbered two years ago. The Tigers haven't allowed a rushing touchdown all season and no team has run for 150 yards against them in the past 11 games.

No 100-yard rushers, either, much less 200-plus.

The Tigers' eight-game winning streak is their longest since a 20- game binge in 1993-94. This year they have mixed in appropriately easy wins against poor teams—Mississippi State, The Citadel and Louisiana-Monroe are a combined 3-12—with inspired performances against LSU and especially Tennessee.

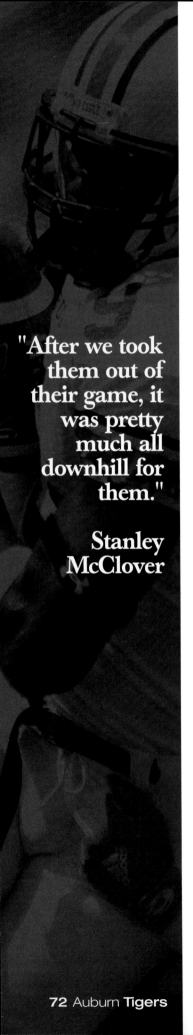

"After we took them out of their game, it was pretty much all downhill for them."

Stanley McClover

Sophomore linebacker Kevin Sears wasn't even around for the 2002 game. But, he said, the coaches began reminding the younger players of that game early in the week, "and aren't going to quit until the game is over with Saturday."

While the Tigers draw on that memory for motivation, Arkansas can get a boost from more recent events in the league. Auburn has beaten Tennessee on the road, Tennessee has won at Georgia and LSU won at Florida.

An Arkansas upset could muddle the league picture even further, keeping the Razorbacks alive in the SEC Western Division and derailing perhaps the last remaining national title contender in the league. Auburn is the SEC's last unbeaten team.

"That's the thing about our league that we talk about every year—anybody can beat anybody on any given Saturday," Arkansas coach Houston Nutt said. "It is a mindset, and a mind game. The one that has their team the most ready and are so focused and ready to go, that makes a lot of difference in the outcome of that game."

This is the most serious obstacle to Auburn's remaining perfect for its Nov. 13 game against No. 12 Georgia.

Arkansas is 0-2 against ranked opponents, but still could gain some confidence from both games. The Razorbacks finished strong after a horrible start in a 45-30 loss to Florida in their last outing two weeks ago and were edged 22-20 by Texas.

They've had an extra week to prepare for opportunity No. 3. Auburn has only been challenged once this season, a 10-9 win over LSU. The Tigers also dealt SEC East frontrunner Tennessee a 34-10 defeat.

"We know this is going to be a big game," Arkansas linebacker Sam Olajabatu said. "A lot of people are talking about Auburn, how they're playing. They deserve to be talked about because they're playing pretty good right now.

"We're just going to come out there and just play our hardest."

Auburn prepares for Arkansas' "Super Matt"

JOHN ZENOR, October 15, 2004

He runs faster than a speeding linebacker, leaps over defensive backs in a single bound and can generally ruin a defense's day.

But can versatile quarterback Matt Jones lift Arkansas to an upset win at No. 4 Auburn on Saturday?

"Super Matt coming in here," Tigers safety Junior Rosegreen said. "I see why they call him Superman because he makes big plays. This is the first time I've ever seen one player that can beat you by himself."

Actually, it will still be Auburn (6-0, 3-0 Southeastern Conference) against Arkansas (3-2, 1-1), not Matt Jones vs. Auburn. But Jones will be wearing a big target on his back instead of a cape, the focal point of the Tigers' defense.

Run, pass, break tackles, outrun defenders. You name it, Jones has been doing it for the Razorbacks for four seasons, and he has Auburn's defenders wary.

"He's basically a one-man show," cornerback Carlos Rogers said. "If we stop him, I think we'll be all right."

Jones is directing the league's top passing offense and leads the SEC in total offense, averaging a whopping 32 yards more than No. 2, Florida quarterback Chris Leak. He's also the leading rusher for the SEC's second-best rushing attack.

Auburn coach Tommy Tuberville calls him "the hottest player in the league" and said the Razorbacks have the best offense his team has faced this season.

"He's just a guy that gives you numerous problems, not just a few," Tuberville said. "He is very dangerous.

"There's not a rhyme or reason to how you play him. You just want to be consistent. He is a gamer. He's probably the

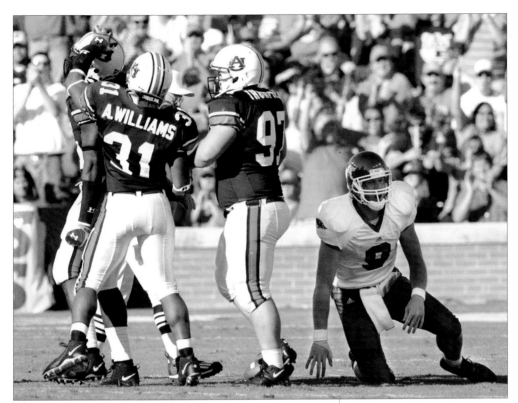

Auburn players react after a sack of Arkansas quarterback Matt Jones during their 38-20 win over the Razorbacks.

more potent one. Quarterback Jason Campbell is rated sixth nationally in passing efficiency and can hand off or throw to running backs Carnell Williams and Ronnie Brown.

The receiving corps also has been making big plays lately.

The Razorbacks have had an extra week to prepare for the Tigers' new West Coast offense, which trails only Arkansas in total yards per game among SEC teams.

"Offensively, they're playing the best they've played since Jason Campbell has been the quarterback," Razorbacks coach Houston Nutt said. "He has two great running backs to hand the ball to and he has some receivers that are very physical.

"Its going to be an all-day type ball game and we just want to be there for four quarters."

No. 4 Auburn 38, Arkansas 20

JOHN ZENOR, October 17, 2004

Jason Campbell was so focused on this game that he couldn't sleep the night before.

Then he turned in the kind of performance that could give defensive coordinators nightmares, throwing for a career-high 297 yards and three touchdowns to lead No. 4 Auburn to a 38-20 rout of Arkansas on Saturday.

With Campbell completing 17 of 19 passes—all in the first three quarters—the Tigers (7-0, 4-0 Southeastern Conference) won their ninth straight game and lived up to their highest ranking in 10 years.

Imagine if he'd actually slept Friday night.

"All night, I couldn't go to sleep," said Campbell, who was 11- of-12 for 210 yards in the first half. "I was just thinking about the game. It was just one of those days one day you'll look back on and be proud of."

The Tigers continue to forge a memorable season as well, scoring on their first five possessions for a 30-0

biggest and also one of the fastest guys in our league."

However, Auburn's quick, swarming defense is formidable, too. The Tigers haven't allowed a rushing touchdown and rank fourth nationally in scoring defense, allowing 7.2 points per game. But they haven't faced the combination of big, mobile, experienced passer that the 6-foot-6 Jones represents—most teams haven't.

"He can do it on the ground with his feet and he can throw the ball real good," Rosegreen said. "He runs good and he's just physical. He makes his other teammates look better. He makes them better by making big plays."

Jones doesn't mind opposing defenses focusing on him. He expects that will lead to opportunities for the lesser-known members of Arkansas' offense—like receiver Steven Harris and running back DeCori Birmingham.

"I think that does open up the offense for our running backs and for our receivers when teams do that," Jones said. "I think we have enough athletes around that if teams want to do that, we're going to have some other players making plays."

Auburn's offense has no shortage of those, presenting a more diverse challenge than the Razorbacks, if not a

Arkansas running back Dedrick Poole is seemingly broken in two after a first down run by Auburn's Junior Rosegreen and Travis Williams in the second quarter.

lead against a team that had given them fits in recent years. Twice in the past three meetings, an unranked Razorback team blew Auburn out.

Not this time.

"Offensively, we just dominated in the first half," coach Tommy Tuberville said. "It was almost a perfect game for us."

And that was too much for Arkansas (3-3, 1-2), which all but fell out of contention in the SEC West.

"When your opponent scores on five consecutive possessions, it makes for a long, long day," Razorbacks coach Houston Nutt said. "It crushes your confidence."

The Razorbacks couldn't muster any consistent offense and quarterback Matt Jones spent much of the game under pressure. The league's total offense leader hurt his groin on the first play of the game, but he was still able to scamper for 54 yards the one time he got free.

"It changed the game," said Jones, who didn't gain any yards on his other three carries. "On the long run, that is six (points) if I am not hurt. I just didn't throw very well."

It was still the most points anybody had scored against Auburn this year.

Ronnie Brown rushed for 101 yards for the Tigers, while Carnell Williams gained 71. Both ran for short touchdowns.

But it was Campbell who continued to drive the offense, making Arkansas pay dearly for loading up against the run and setting an Auburn record for completion percentage in a game. His highest total in his first 33 starts was 270 yards against Alabama last year, and he topped that in the third quarter before the offense went to the run to protect its lead.

"The main thing we say every week is we want to beat teams to the punch," Campbell said. "We want to get off to a fast start."

The Razorbacks got a late touchdown set up by an interception against backup quarterback Brandon Cox.

The Tigers had said all week they wouldn't let Jones beat them, running or passing. The 54-yard burst briefly made him the SEC's top career rushing quarterback, but even that didn't hold up.

Jones got sacked for a 9-yard loss on the next drive, pushing him back into a tie with John Bond of Mississippi State at 2,280 yards. Jones was 12-of-27 passing for 189 yards with two TDs.

The Tigers outgained Arkansas 522-337.

"After we took them out of their game, it was pretty much all downhill for them," defensive end Stanley McClover said.

Campbell was nearly perfect in the first half. He hit Devin Aromashodu for a 67-yard score after a reverse flea-flicker on the game's third play, and hit Courtney Taylor for a 30-yard score later in the first quarter.

"That was a play everyone's been talking about all week," Campbell said of the trick play. "Everyone on the team wanted to run it. It hardly ever works in practice."

Aromashodu had four catches for a career-high 102 yards.

Jones threw nine consecutive incompletions after starting out 4- of-4, but then threatened to bring Arkansas back into the game. He hit Chris Baker for a 19-yard touchdown late in the half to make it 30-7 and found Steven Harris for a 61-yarder on the opening drive of the third quarter.

Campbell put it away with a 19-yard TD pass to Ben Obomanu, his final throw.

John Vaughn missed an extra point for Auburn in the first half, ending the team's SEC record streak of 209 straight.

	Arkansas	Auburn
First Downs	15	26
3rd-Down Efficiency	4-12-33%	6-10-60%
4th-Down Efficiency	0-2-0%	0-0--%
Total net yards	337	522
Net yards rushing	128	225
Net yards passing	209	297
Penalties-yards	9-59	5-44
Time of Possession	23:56	36:40

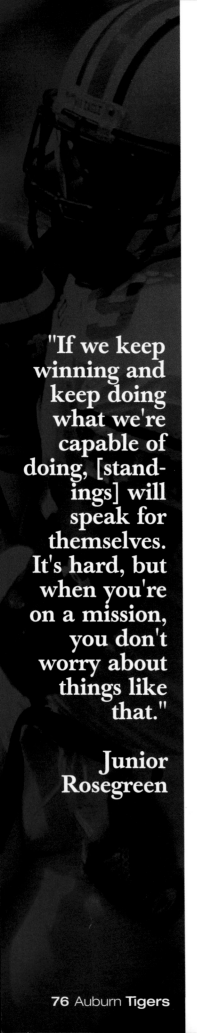

"If we keep winning and keep doing what we're capable of doing, [standings] will speak for themselves. It's hard, but when you're on a mission, you don't worry about things like that."

Junior Rosegreen

No. 3 Auburn 42, Kentucky 10

October 23, 2004

Jones: Auburn potential title contender

JOHN ZENOR, October 17, 2004

There was some national championship talk going on in the locker room at Auburn's Jordan-Hare Stadium.

The visitors' locker room, that is.

The third-ranked Tigers refused to engage in such ambitious talk after dismantling Arkansas 38-20 on Saturday, but Razorbacks quarterback Matt Jones had no such qualms.

"They have a chance to do something special this year," Jones said. "They have a chance to go to the SEC championship game and possibly the national championship game."

With the initial Bowl Championship Series standings due out Monday, national title talk is perhaps premature. What's not at all premature is the likelihood that the Tigers (7-0, 4-0 Southeastern Conference) will be playing for the league title in Atlanta.

Only games against Kentucky (1-5, 0-3) and at Mississippi (3-4, 2-2) are on the horizon before No. 10 Georgia visits on Nov. 13.

The Razorbacks (3-3, 1-2) were the chief contender for the SEC West crown after the Tigers beat LSU 10-9, their only close game this season. Every other team in the division has at least two league losses.

So how about those BCS standings?

"There's no reason to worry about that," Auburn defensive back Junior Rosegreen said. "If we keep winning and keep doing what we're capable of doing, those things will speak for themselves.

"It's hard, but when you're on a mission, you don't worry about things like that."

Auburn can draw plenty of confidence from the way quarterback Jason Campbell, tailback Ronnie Brown and the defense are playing.

Campbell was a pristine 17-of-19 for a career-high 297 yards and three touchdowns against Arkansas. It was the highest completion percentage any Auburn quarterback had managed in a game, but they weren't all high percentage passes.

Campbell had a 67-yard TD pass to Devin Aromashodu off a flea flicker, a 30-yarder to Courtney Taylor and a 19-yarder to Ben Obomanu.

"I told Jason before the game it's not as important how many you hit, but that you hit the right ones," offensive coordinator Al Borges said. "I didn't know he would hit them all."

Auburn's Marquies Gunn reacts after sacking Kentucky quarterback Andre Woodson in the second quarter of the Tigers' 42-10 rout of the Wildcats.

Auburn Tigers

scores of the teams ranked ahead of them—Miami, Oklahoma and Southern California.

He was frustrated by the Hurricanes' 41-38 scare against Louisville Thursday night, but the Tigers vaulted over Miami in the rankings anyway.

"We were kind of mad about that game," Rogers said. "They should have won it. But at the same time, our opportunity is going to come."

On the flip side: "Lose once and we're out of there."

Auburn moves from turmoil to triumph

JOHN ZENOR, October 19, 2004

Auburn bungled an attempt to oust its coach, and three of its stars nearly left early for the NFL.

Almost a year later, the Tigers are unbeaten. And coach Tommy Tuberville and top players Carnell Williams, Ronnie Brown and Carlos Rogers are the main reasons No. 3 Auburn (7-0) is in the running for the national championship.

"Everybody wants to say coach has got to be laughing," Tuberville said. "I've been in this business 29 years. What happened last year, I've forgotten about. I'm glad it's worked out the way it did."

Couldn't have worked out much better so far.

Auburn has been the Southeastern Conference's best team this season, finally living up to the hype and acclaim that overwhelmed the Tigers in 2003.

Last year's free-fall from a preseason No. 6 ranking has been replaced by a steady, unrelenting climb up the rankings.

That woefully inconsistent offense? It's leading the league.

> "We didn't play our best game, and we won by 32 points. That just says a lot about our team coming together."
>
> **Ronnie Brown**

Brown gained 101 yards on 15 carries, his second straight 100- yard performance off the bench. Starter Carnell Williams gained 71 yards but coach Tommy Tuberville reserved his biggest praise for their blocking not their running.

"It's tough for somebody to defend what we're doing," Tuberville said.

While the offense was racking up 522 yards, the defense allowed two big plays from Jones—a 54-yard run and a 61-yard touchdown pass to Steven Harris—but little else to the league's top offense. Jones was hampered by a groin injury much of the game.

"I think we're playing good right now," defensive end Stanley McClover said. "We've still got a long way to go.

"If everyone keeps getting better and everyone plays hard, we've got a chance to be a great team."

Cornerback Carlos Rogers admits it's getting harder and harder not to check out

(above) Auburn's Carnell Williams is tackled by Kentucky's Muhammad Abdullah and Mike Williams after a first down run in the first quarter. (right) Auburn's Courtney Taylor catches the ball in between Kentucky defenders Muhammad Abdullah and Marcus McClinton, left.

Auburn **Tigers**

The defense that lost three starting linemen and two All-SEC linebackers? It has allowed the second fewest points in the nation, just nine per game, and is the only Division I-A team that hasn't allowed a rushing touchdown.

And with the Tigers fourth in this week's first Bowl Championship Series standings, Tuberville is more likely to get a lifetime contract than to lose his job.

Then-interim President William Walker was forced to retain Tuberville after an expedition he led to interview Louisville's Bobby Petrino two days before last year's Alabama game became public, angering Auburn fans and alumni.

The university's administration had egg on its face. The football team still had its coach. And the Tigers have won nine straight since Walker & Co. boarded the plane to Kentucky.

"We know about everything that went down with our coach last year, and we know how people downed us last year because they were expecting more," receiver Courtney Taylor said. "We just don't want to be in that position anymore.

"I feel like we were at the bottom of the barrel, and now we're just trying to climb our way out."

The Tigers have risen to the occasion this season, including a 34- 10 rout at Tennessee.

They've only been challenged once, but answered with a gutsy game- winning drive against LSU. Leading that drive was Jason Campbell, a formerly maligned quarterback whose turnaround has been about as dramatic as Auburn's.

Thriving in a West Coast system implemented by new offensive coordinator Al Borges, Campbell is the nation's fourth-rated passer with 13 touchdown passes, only two interceptions and a 67.6 percent completion rate.

"Its just great to finally hear your name mentioned," Campbell said. "Through all of the things I've been through here, there's finally an opportunity to have success."

Tailbacks Brown and Williams have been solid, too. They rank fifth and sixth in the SEC in rushing yards per game, combining for 1,153 yards.

When that pair and Rogers, a cornerback, opted to return for their senior seasons, it had a big impact on the Tigers _ on and off the field.

"The thing that we lacked was confidence," Tuberville said. "With these guys coming back and believing in what we're doing, I think it helped everybody."

Tuberville has taken pains to make sure his team doesn't get overconfident. He seldom mentions the opposing team by name to his players during game week, emphasizing Auburn's own execution.

The philosophy behind that: "Our gameplan's going to be dictated to ourselves. We're not going to let them dictate to us."

Every player and coach sits in on the weekly special teams meetings, whether they play on special teams or not. And many of the top players do, including Williams, Brown and Rogers.

"By doing that, we're trying to create more of a team concept," Tuberville said.

And he's not worrying about his job security anymore. Tuberville said many fans rallied around him after the Petrino episode, and that he finally thinks Auburn has its "ducks in a row."

Interim President Ed Richardson has said his coach will be "rewarded for doing an outstanding job" at season's end.

"I'm not laughing behind the scenes or gloating or saying I told you so, any of those things," Tuberville said. "I'm glad to be here.

"I think the only way this job can be done is both sides have to forgive and forget. As long as we're doing what's best for Auburn, I'm fine with it."

No. 3 Auburn 42, Kentucky 10

JOHN ZENOR, October 23, 2004

Auburn is no longer judging its performances by the final score.

Carnell Williams rushed for 149 yards and two touchdowns, and the No. 3 Tigers allowed only 110 yards in a 42-10 rout of Kentucky on Saturday. But Williams wasn't impressed.

"It kind of showed you how talented this team is," said Williams, who had his first 100-yard performance in six

Auburn's Ronnie Brown leaps over teammate Danny Lindsey and Kentucky defender Kamaal Ahmad.

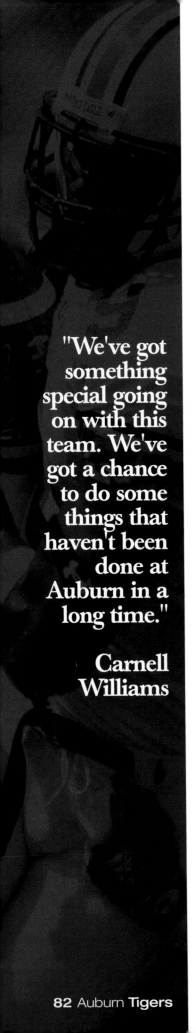

"We've got something special going on with this team. We've got a chance to do some things that haven't been done at Auburn in a long time."

Carnell Williams

games. "We didn't play too good at all."

The end result was the same for the Tigers (8-0, 5-0 Southeastern Conference), who began the week by debuting at No. 4 in the Bowl Championship Series standings.

They overpowered the league's worst defense to overcome a stretch of sloppy play, and rode the nation's No. 2 scoring defense to a fifth straight blowout.

Auburn will take it, pretty or not.

"We didn't play our best game, and we won by 32 points," said Ronnie Brown, who scored on runs of 12 and 17 yards. "That just says a lot about our team coming together."

It also says plenty about the Wildcats (1-6, 0-4), who have dropped five consecutive games and 14 in a row against the Tigers.

Williams, who needed only 17 carries for his third 100-yard game of the season, scored on runs of 1 and 9 yards in the first quarter as Auburn opened up a 21-0 lead in the first 10:29.

Jason Campbell completed 11 of 15 passes for 127 yards but this game belonged to the running backs and the defense, and neither disappointed. All three offensive stars sat out the fourth quarter.

Redshirt freshman Andre' Woodson was sacked seven times in his first start at quarterback for Kentucky with Shane Boyd sidelined by a shoulder injury. He was 14-of-26 passing for only 73 yards and lost two fumbles, the second returned for a late 15-yard score by Kevis Burnam.

Well, he can't say Quentin Groves didn't warn him.

"I told him the first time I hit him, 'I'm going to be back here all day, baby,'" said Groves, who had three sacks and forced both fumbles.

The Tigers held Kentucky to 37 yards on 36 rushes, constantly penetrating the line to harass Woodson and bury the runners.

"I could have played a lot better, but they are the No. (3) team in the nation and they showed why," Woodson said.

Auburn scored touchdowns on its first three possessions after opening at Kentucky's 29, 35 and 19 with help from two short punts and a fumble by Woodson.

"It was one of the worst starts to a football game that I have ever been part of," said Wildcats coach Rich Brooks, calling his offense "skittish."

Then the Tigers got sloppy and led only 21-7 at the half.

Rafael Little's 3-yard touchdown run on fourth-and-1 in the second quarter was the first rushing score the Tigers have given up this season.

Auburn coach Tommy Tuberville then inserted the No. 2 offense, and backup quarterback Brandon Cox promptly was intercepted by Antoine Huffman at the Tigers 40. The defense saved them by forcing a punt.

However, Auburn's last drive of the half ended with two consecutive penalties—one negating a touchdown pass to Courtney Taylor—and a sack.

Campbell fumbled a snap from backup center Steven Ross—subbing for an injured Jeremy Ingle—on the second play of the third quarter. Kentucky answered with Taylor Begley's 37-yard field goal.

That got the Tigers going again.

Auburn responded by moving 80 yards on nine plays with Brown scoring on a 17-yarder and the rout was on again. Campbell converted a fourth-and-3 with a 7-yard pass to Taylor on the previous play and Williams scampered 36 yards into Wildcats territory.

Kentucky's leading rusher, Tony Dixon, aggravated an ankle injury early and didn't return. Brooks said he and Boyd are out indefinitely.

Tuberville found plenty of fault in the Tigers' effort, including 10 penalties for 90 yards.

"When you are in control of the game like that, there is not a whole lot of emotion or enthusiasm," he said.

Auburn's Tuberville lobbies for title chances

JOHN ZENOR, October 26, 2004

Tommy Tuberville would be shocked if a Southeastern Conference team went undefeated, won the league title game and failed to get a shot at the national title.

But it could happen—to Tuberville's Auburn Tigers.

The third-ranked Tigers (8-0) are fourth in the Bowl Championship Series standings. Southern California has the top spot, followed by Oklahoma and Miami. For Auburn, winning out might not be enough to play in the Orange Bowl for the BCS title.

"I'd be shocked if a team ever goes through their schedule in the SEC and wins an SEC championship game, be 12-0 and not have an opportunity to win the national championship," Tuberville said. "I think you can just look at the teams in our league, it's very demanding."

Auburn can lock up a spot in the SEC championship game with a win Saturday at Mississippi, owning the West division title before its first open date next week. The Tigers then host No. 10 Georgia and visit Alabama, so while a spot in the league title game seems to be a lock, a perfect record is far from assured.

Just in case, Tuberville started his lobbying.

"LSU won the (BCS) national championship last year and had a loss in the conference—at home," Tuberville said. "If we would have an opportunity to win all the way through, I don't think there would be much doubt we would have an opportunity.

"There would probably be some people who would think I'd be wrong about that, but that's the reason you have polls and the BCS to determine who has fought the toughest battle."

Auburn almost certainly needs at least one of the higher-rated teams to lose.

A rematch against either the Volunteers or Georgia would await for the league title game in Atlanta. Oklahoma also must survive a conference title game in the Big 12, while Miami still faces No. 13 Virginia on Nov. 13 and No. 22 Virginia Tech on Dec. 4. USC doesn't have a ranked opponent left.

Tuberville said for Auburn to win the SEC championship and not get at least a shot at a national title, "I'd say there would be something wrong with the system if that happened. The Big 12 playing the championship game, (it's the) same thing. That's just added pressure and a tougher schedule obviously."

Auburn won its only national championship in 1957. The last SEC team to win every regular-season game and not get a shot at the national title: Auburn in 1993, thanks to NCAA probation.

"We've got something special going on with this team," tailback Carnell Williams said. "We've got a chance to do some things that haven't been done at Auburn in a long time."

Quarterback Jason Campbell said the Tigers are getting "addicted to winning."

"You just have that urge and want to win all the time," he said. "I think that's what this team's got right now. At the same time, it's been a great ride."

Lest they get ahead of themselves, the team called a players- only meeting Sunday. The subject: Focus.

"We kind of sat down and Jason Campbell talked about how we just need to stay focused," Williams said. "We're going to have a lot of stuff thrown our way, with the SEC championship, national rankings, things like that."

Defensive end Bret Eddins characterized the national championship talk as "interesting."

"But I think everybody on the team realizes that we're one game away from being out of that picture," Eddins said.

	Kentucky	Auburn
First Downs	9	17
3rd-Down Efficiency	2-17-12%	4-13-31%
4th-Down Efficiency	2-3-67%	2-2-100%
Total net yards	110	337
Net yards rushing	37	210
Net yards passing	73	127
Penalties-yards	10-57	10-90
Time of Possession	30:35	29:25

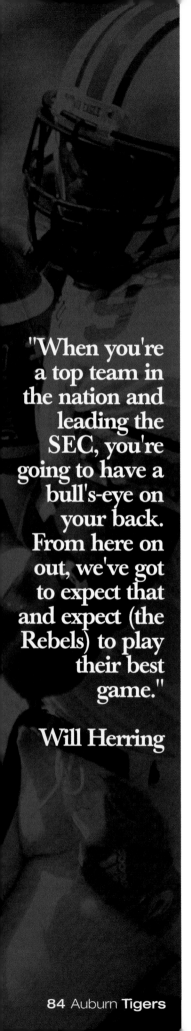

"When you're a top team in the nation and leading the SEC, you're going to have a bull's-eye on your back. From here on out, we've got to expect that and expect (the Rebels) to play their best game."

Will Herring

No. 3 Auburn 35, Ole Miss 14

October 30, 2004

Auburn focused on clinching spot in SEC championship

JOEDY McCREARY, October 29, 2004

Tommy Tuberville returns to Mississippi with a trip to Atlanta on the line, and he's bringing his best Auburn team yet.

The third-ranked Tigers need one win to lock up a spot in the Southeastern Conference championship game before their first off week of the season, and all they have to do is win Saturday at Mississippi—where Tuberville hasn't lost since leaving Oxford for Auburn six years ago.

"That is what we wanted to do early—to have an opportunity to say, 'Hey, we've got another game at the end of the year, and October hasn't even come to a close' would be a pretty good accomplishment out of these guys," Tuberville said.

Auburn (8-0, 5-0) is one win from clinching its third appearance in the league championship game in Atlanta. The Tigers won or shared three of the past four Western Division crowns, but are 0-2 in league title games since the conference split into divisions in 1992.

They pledged not to get caught up in Bowl Championship Series talk, a possible undefeated season or a shot at the school's first national title since 1957. The Tigers emphasized focus at a players- only meeting earlier this week.

"When you're a top team in the nation and leading the SEC, you're going to have a bull's-eye on your back," safety Will Herring said. "From here on out, we've got to expect that and expect (the Rebels) to play their best game."

Ole Miss (3-4, 2-2) isn't thinking about spoiling Auburn's dream season but saving its own.

The Rebels need wins in three of their final four games just to qualify for a third straight bowl, and they close the season against Arkansas, LSU and Mississippi State.

"We're trying to work on our own season," coach David Cutcliffe said. "Auburn is a terrific football team and has earned every accolade they've received this year, but we are worried about ourselves more than their situation."

On paper, it looks like a mismatch.

Auburn leads the conference in scoring and total offense, and scoring defense. The Tigers have two of the league's top running backs, Carnell

---

Auburn running back Carnell Williams sprints past a Mississippi defender on his way to a 4th quarter 29-yard touchdown run.

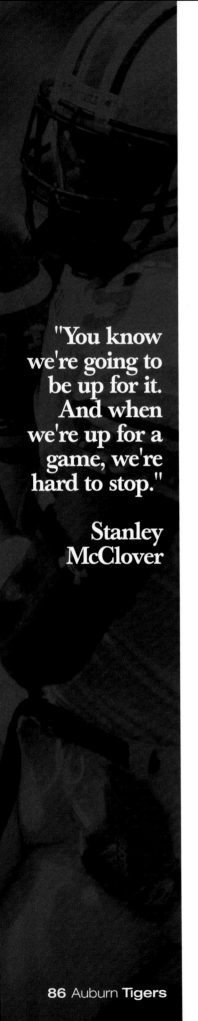

"You know we're going to be up for it. And when we're up for a game, we're hard to stop."

Stanley McClover

Williams and Ronnie Brown, and its most efficient quarterback, Mississippi native Jason Campbell.

"This is the best Auburn team we've faced in the six years I've been here," Cutcliffe said.

Meanwhile, Ole Miss is in the bottom half of the league in virtually every significant statistical category.

"You know we're going to be up for it," Auburn defensive end Stanley McClover said. "And when we're up for a game, we're hard to stop."

With so much at stake, Tuberville isn't getting caught up in another return to Oxford, where he's 2-0 as a visitor since he left for Auburn after the 1998 regular season.

Besides, he isn't convinced that anyone back at Ole Miss remembers him.

"All the students, unless they're on the six-year plan I was on at Southern Arkansas, they're all gone," Tuberville said.

No. 3 Auburn 35, Mississippi 14

JOEDY McCREARY, October 31, 2004

Jason Campbell and Auburn earned some rest. After winning nine games in nine grueling weeks, the Tigers have something to celebrate—and some extra time to party.

Campbell rushed for two touchdowns and threw for another, and No. 3 Auburn earned a spot in the Southeastern Conference championship game with a 35-14 win over Mississippi on Saturday night.

"We were running on fumes _ our players were pretty tired," Auburn coach Tommy Tuberville said. "They scraped enough to get us a win."

Especially Campbell. The league's most efficient quarterback was 11-of-22 for 234 yards and had two 1-yard touchdown runs for the Tigers (9-0, 6-0), who scored 28 points after halftime to lock up the SEC West title before their first off week of the season.

The Tigers have won or shared four of the past five division crowns, but are 0-2 in league championship games since the SEC split into divisions in 1992.

Some Auburn players celebrated their latest achievement by leaping into the orange-clad section of the crowd—a la the Lambeau Leap—and dancing in the end zone as flashbulbs popped in the stands.

"To finish it out in nine games says a lot about this team," said Campbell, a Mississippi native.

Florida beat the Tigers 28-6 in their most recent SEC title game appearance in 2000, when Campbell and some current Auburn seniors were freshmen.

"We would get to the end of the season and have the opportunity to go to Atlanta, and something just wouldn't work out," Campbell said.

This time, Auburn will play either No. 10 Georgia or No. 11 Tennessee in the league title game in Atlanta—and more importantly, the Tigers can keep dreaming of a perfect season and national title.

The Tigers are off next week before hosting Georgia and playing at Alabama. The SEC championship game is Dec. 4.

"We won't think about the BCS," Tuberville said. "Georgia and Alabama are enough to think about."

Tuberville hasn't lost in three games as a visitor to Oxford. He coached Ole Miss for four years but bolted for Auburn in 1998.

Ronnie Brown ran for 100 yards and a touchdown, and Carnell Williams had 96 yards rushing and a 29-yard TD run.

Campbell's 1-yard sneak with 0:26 left in the first half gave Auburn a 7-0 lead.

Mississippi defenders try to block a second quarter pass by Auburn quarterback Jason Campbell.

His second short touchdown run early in the fourth quarter restored the Tigers' 14-point lead.

"You're having to be ready for the run all the time and the pass as well," Ole Miss defensive back Travis Johnson said. "They're a great team, and you've just got to stay focused in order to beat them."

Auburn never trailed, but the Rebels were thinking upset early in the fourth. Ethan Flatt's 25-yard touchdown pass to Taye Biddle pulled Ole Miss within seven.

That didn't last long. Williams set up Campbell's second TD when he returned a punt 38 yards to the Ole Miss 25. The Rebels didn't threaten the rest of the way.

Flatt was 12-of-20 for 225 yards and two touchdowns for Ole Miss (3-5, 2-3), which is in serious danger of missing the postseason. The Rebels must beat Arkansas, LSU and Mississippi State just to qualify for their third straight bowl.

"We know what the circumstances are," Ole Miss coach David Cutcliffe said. "The only way to approach this is to get through the open date and prepare well for Arkansas."

Flatt's 64-yard touchdown pass to Bill Flowers pulled the Rebels to 14-7, but Campbell answered with a 9-yard scoring pass to Courtney Taylor.

Ole Miss managed to keep it close in the first half because the Tigers seemed out of sync. Campbell threw seven straight incompletions during one ineffective stretch, and Auburn failed to score on a first-and-goal from the 2.

"It says something when you can win on the road in this conference and not play at full strength," Tuberville said. "We just made too many mistakes late in the third and fourth quarter."

But Auburn was too fast and too strong for the Rebels, who once again couldn't beat their former coach at home.

Auburn's Brown no longer just that other tailback

JOHN ZENOR, November 4, 2004

It could have been Ronnie Brown's breakaway run, a chance to step out of Carnell Williams' shadow at Auburn and head to the NFL.

Instead, he decided to stick around for his senior season, surprising even some of his friends.

"At first, a lot of people were like, 'What are you doing?'" the Tigers tailback recalls with a smile.

Turns out he was doing the right thing. Brown has been an integral part of No. 3 Auburn's impressive surge into the national championship hunt with a 9-0 start, turning heads with his remarkable versatility for a 230-pound running back.

Here's three surefire ways to emerge from the more heralded Williams' shadow: Run, block, catch.

Brown is the Southeastern Conference's No. 7 rusher with 689 yards in eight games and the team's No. 2 receiver with 18 catches for 176 yards. And guess who threw the key downfield block that sprung Williams for a 57-yard catch against Mississippi last week?

Yep, Brown.

"We've always known how good Ronnie is," center Jeremy Ingle said. "He's one of the best backs in the country—top three, in my opinion. He's the total package, he really is."

Brown and Williams both were projected as likely second-round draft picks after last season, and Brown already had his degree in communication. He came back anyway, and his stock almost certainly has gone up.

"Ronnie Brown loves college football," Auburn coach Tommy Tuberville said. "Both of these guys just wanted to come

---

Auburn football coach Tommy Tuberville argues with an official in the second quarter.

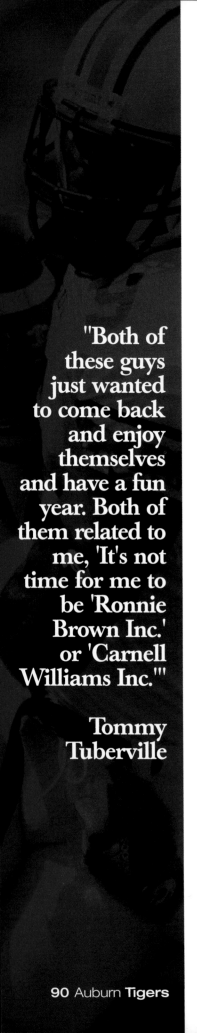

"Both of these guys just wanted to come back and enjoy themselves and have a fun year. Both of them related to me, 'It's not time for me to be 'Ronnie Brown Inc.' or 'Carnell Williams Inc.'"

Tommy Tuberville

back and enjoy themselves and have a fun year. Both of them related to me, 'It's not time for me to be 'Ronnie Brown Inc.' or 'Carnell Williams Inc.'

"They wanted to come back and enjoy college life and maybe improve on what they were doing and maybe improve next year for the NFL draft."

Williams has been superb, too, running for 862 yards, fourth in the league. But Brown's 7.3 yards per carry ranks first among the SEC's top 10 runners, and he has four 100-yard games compared to three for Williams.

The pair have lined up in the backfield together at times and even at receiver. Each could rush for 1,000 yards this season.

Plus, the Tigers have clinched a spot in the SEC championship game. They have an open date this weekend, before games against top rivals Georgia and Alabama.

"This is some of the stuff that you're dreaming about," Brown said. "I really didn't expect all of this when I decided to come back, but it's been great."

Last year he tied for second on the team in rushing with junior college transfer Brandon Jacobs, who transferred again after the season.

Yet he was still well regarded by NFL scouts and personnel officials, who indicated he could go as high as the second round. Again the voices: "Things didn't go so good for you last year. What makes you think they're going to get better?" Brown said friends asked him.

He's never known exactly what to expect before a season.

In 2000, an injury forced him to redshirt after playing sparingly in three games behind SEC player of the year Rudi Johnson.

Johnson left early for the NFL but Auburn signed Williams, Alabama's Mr. Football and one of the nation's top tail-

back prospects. Brown opened the next season as the starter, but soon was replaced by Williams.

In 2002, Brown replaced an injured Williams midway through the season and wound up with 1,008 yards, including 184 against Penn State in a bowl game.

"It's been kind of weird," said Brown, who has had an assortment of injuries. "Most of the time you come in and play and then things just kind of go up. But I had to face a little adversity from time to time. I kind of appreciate those times, just looking where I'm at now and the situation I'm in now. It's kind of paid off."

Running backs coach Eddie Gran would have understood if Brown had shown up in his office griping about lack of carries, but says it didn't happen.

"He's never been in my office (complaining) one time," Gran said. "If anybody had a gripe, it would have been him. He could have come to my office and said, 'Coach, why am I not getting carries? What's the deal here?'

"Never. Not one time. In our society, that doesn't happen very often."

	Auburn	Mississippi
First Downs	18	20
3rd-Down Efficiency	3-11-27%	4-14-29%
4th-Down Efficiency	0-1-0%	0-2-0%
Total net yards	439	433
Net yards rushing	205	147
Net yards passing	234	286
Penalties-yards	8-55	10-104
Time of Possession	23:57	36:30

Auburn defensive end Doug Langenfeld waves his school's banner following their victory.

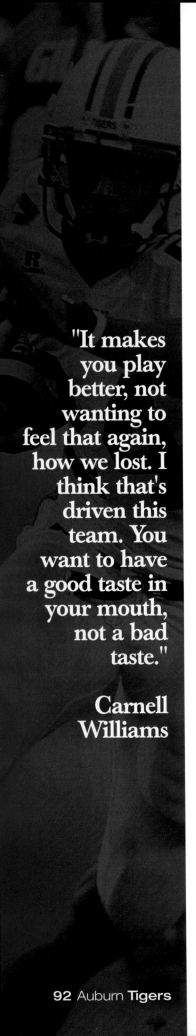

"It makes you play better, not wanting to feel that again, how we lost. I think that's driven this team. You want to have a good taste in your mouth, not a bad taste."

Carnell Williams

No. 3 Auburn 24, No. 8 Georgia 6

November 13, 2004

Auburn using tough 2003 loss as springboard

JOHN ZENOR, November 8, 2004

Carnell Williams gives a brutally candid assessment of Auburn's last run-in with Georgia."It was disgusting," he said.

So disgusting, in fact, that the Tigers apparently decided they wanted to lose that losing feeling. They've won 11 consecutive games since that 26-7 humbling on Nov. 15, 2003, when the offense was a mess and the defense wasn't good enough to compensate.

The third-ranked Tigers (9-0, 6-0 Southeastern Conference) haven't had much cause since then to revisit that painful game. Now they do: Saturday's rematch with the eighth-ranked Bulldogs (8-1, 6- 1), with Auburn's national championship hopes on the line.

"We didn't play too well and we basically got outmanned, outphysicalled," said Williams, Auburn's leading rusher. "They just beat us in every phase of the game. I felt like after that game, we didn't want to lose that way anymore."

That loss dropped the preseason league favorites to 6-5, prompting Auburn officials to consider replacing coach Tommy Tuberville. It supplied a perfect illustration of the issues that plagued the Tigers a year ago: no offensive identity, too many mistakes and not enough fight.

This Auburn team provides a stark contrast to the 2003 version that floundered around Sanford Stadium. The Tigers couldn't run much and, surprisingly, hardly tried.

Tailbacks Williams and Ronnie Brown had two rushes apiece before halftime, putting much of the load on quarterback Jason Campbell, who struggled then but has been terrific ever since.

The defeat followed a disheartening loss to Mississippi.

"It was just a disaster," said Campbell, whose fourth-quarter interception was returned 99 yards by Odell Thurman. "To get beat the way we did last year wasn't Auburn football. It wasn't us. It had a lot to do with how we got beat by Ole Miss the week before that."

Now, Campbell is the nation's third-rated passer and the team has deftly mixed the run and pass under new offensive coordinator Al Borges.

The defense has allowed the second-fewest points in the nation, behind Wisconsin, and the offense leads the league in scoring.

The resurgence began immediately after

Auburn's Carnell Williams breaks away from Georgia's Brian Jordan as he returns a punt in the thrid quarter. TheTigers made amends for last year's loss with a 24-6 victory.

(left) Auburn's Carnell Williams throws a touchdown pass in the second quarter. (above) Williams, in his more familiar role as a running back, slips past Georgia's Arnold Harrison during the first quarter.

Georgia, Auburn stars remain in school with no regrets

PAUL NEWBERRY, November 11, 2004

David Pollack kept going back and forth, trying to decide whether he wanted to play on Saturdays or Sundays.

The lure of college life was strong. So was the idea of playing in the NFL. Finally, Georgia's star defensive end came to a decision that seems a bit out of place in today's world.

One more year with the Bulldogs. Sundays could wait.

"That's the best decision I ever made," Pollack said, without a hint of regret about returning for his senior season. "And not just for football. For my life, too."

He wasn't alone. Down at Auburn, star running backs Carnell Williams and Ronnie Brown, along with cornerback Carlos Rogers, all decided to hang around for their senior years.

Even Pollack's best friend, Georgia quarterback David Greene, had a chance to enter the draft. He never seriously considered it.

Now, all five of these seniors—yep, they still have those in college football—are at the forefront for one of the biggest Saturdays of the season.

The No. 8 Bulldogs (8-1) will try to bolster their hopes of reaching the Bowl Championship Series when they travel to Auburn, where the third-ranked Tigers (9-0) are right in the thick of the national championship race.

It's the oldest rivalry in the Deep South, a worthy platform to show all those underclassmen that staying in school can pay off—even when there's no actual dollars involved.

"It's not just good for us or Georgia or our conference," Auburn coach Tommy Tuberville said. "It's great for college football to see guys come back for their senior year and have success. I think all these guys will have improved their stature and matured toward the next level with the way they've played."

No argument there.

Pollack, who had 14 sacks as a sophomore, dropped off to 7 1/2 last season while facing almost constant double-teaming. Still, he was told by NFL scouts that he would be drafted somewhere in the first round.

the Georgia loss, with wins over Alabama and in the Music City Bowl against Wisconsin.

"It makes you play better, not wanting to feel that again, how we lost, how we played," Campbell said. "I think that's driven this team. You want to have a good taste in your mouth, not a bad taste.

"It's not good when you walk around and hear things. What we were hearing last year was just awful."

Bad as that was, Campbell said it still didn't top the 2002 Georgia game for sheer agony. That's when David Greene hit Michael Johnson for a touchdown on fourth-and-15 for a 24-21 win at Jordan- Hare Stadium.

That loss bumped Auburn from the rankings and ended their hopes of an SEC Western Division title.

"I think it hurt us the most out of all the close ones we lost because it would have given us a chance to go to Atlanta and play in the SEC championship," Campbell said. "It hurt because it was a fourth-down play.

"He caught it in the back of the end zone, one step from being out. The way we lost it, that kind of hurt."

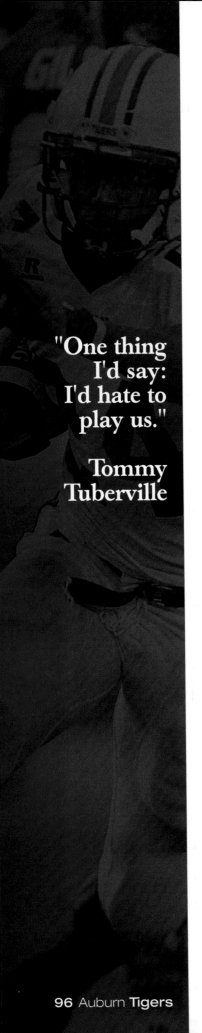

"One thing
I'd say:
I'd hate to
play us."

Tommy
Tuberville

It wasn't enough to lure him away, and he'll certainly go higher than he would have last April. Despite the continued double-teams, Pollack already has matched his sack total from a year ago, setting a school record with 31 in his career.

Plus, he's caused tremendous havoc up front, creating space for his teammates such as Odell Thurman and Thomas Davis to make plays. Not surprisingly, Georgia ranks among the top 15 nationally in both points allowed and total defense.

Along the way, Pollack has gained a level of maturity that prepared him for the real world—a world he wasn't ready to face a year ago.

"I grew up more in the past year than at any time in my life," Pollack said. "I learned to cook more. I learned to clean more. I can do my own clothes. I don't eat fried foods anymore. It's just a matter of growing up."

For Auburn's trio, the decision to stay also worked out just fine.

Start with Williams and Brown, who have a job-sharing arrangement that benefits them both. Cadillac ranks fourth in the Southeastern Conference with 862 yards, including nine touchdowns. Brown is averaging 7.3 yards per carry, has scored seven TDs and ranks just behind his teammate in the SEC's rushing stats (689 yards).

Rogers, meanwhile, is a semifinalist for the Jim Thorpe Award as the nation's top defensive back and one of the leaders for a unit that has surrendered just 9.7 points a game—second fewest in the nation.

By hanging around, they could be part of one of the greatest seasons in school history.

"I feel that was one of the best decisions I've ever made in my life, to come back to Auburn University," Williams said. "Just to be a part of what we're doing and the atmosphere around here and things like that, I'm very happy with the decision that I've made."

His happiness doesn't figure to wane on draft day.

Williams and Brown were both projected as possible second-round picks if they had left school early. With the way they've played as seniors, there's a chance they'll be in line for the really big first-round money.

It's the same situation for Rogers, who likely would have gone somewhere between the second and fourth round this past April. By coming back for another year of school, he might crack the first round, too.

"Looking back on it, I'm glad I did it," Brown said. "Some of the things we've done this season, I'm glad I didn't miss any of it. I'm looking forward to the future, too."

Ahh, the future. When the season ends, another group of NFL wannabes—including Georgia's Davis and Thurman—will have to decide: stay in school or go to the pros?

Even though it worked out for Pollack, he doesn't expect his path to become a trend. Some players face financial hardships at home, making it hard for them to turn down a paycheck.

"I don't have any kids. A lot of guys in college have kids," Pollack said. "And I was blessed. My parents aren't hurting for money. I'm sure if my parents were in dire need of money, I probably would have left."

Davis has a son who turns 1 next month and is leaning toward the NFL, though he will certainly listen to any advice Pollack has to offer about staying in school.

"Guys have things in their life they need to accomplish, they need to handle," Davis said. "I'm a different person. My situation is totally different."

In other words, let's enjoy this while we can.

No. 3 Auburn in one of its biggest games against No. 8 Georgia

JOHN ZENOR, November 12, 2004

A victory by third-ranked Auburn over No. 8 Georgia would leave the Tigers in a strong

Georgia's Reggie Brown tries to fend off Auburn's Carlos Rogers after making a catch .

position to challenge for the national championship.

So, Auburn is approaching the matchup Saturday at Jordan-Hare Stadium as if it were a bowl game. The Tigers haven't made a serious run at the title since they beat Michigan in the 1984 Sugar Bowl.

"The national championship was in play in that game," said longtime Auburn athletic director David Housel.

It's in play again. The Tigers (9-0, 6-0 Southeastern Conference) are hoping for a happier ending this time. Despite a 9-7 victory over Sugar Bowl victory over Michigan, Auburn was leapfrogged by fourth-ranked Miami after the top two teams lost their bowl games.

But Auburn is faced with the reality that an even an SEC title and a perfect season would make the Tigers nothing more than spectators watching top-ranked Southern California and No. 2 Oklahoma duke it out for the national championship in the Orange Bowl.

That detracts little from the Georgia game, clearly one of the biggest ever here because of the high stakes and coming so deep into the season.

"It's going to be crazy and I'm ready for it," defensive end Stanley McClover said.

The game is certainly big for the Bulldogs (8-1, 6-1) as well. They are still in contention to play Auburn in the SEC Championship game if they win their final two games and Tennessee loses to either Vanderbilt or Kentucky.

A win also would be a big boost to Georgia's hopes of making a Bowl Championship Series game. A loss effectively ends that chance.

"This is the biggest game of the year," Georgia defensive end David Pollack said. "It is the next game. It is obvious what is at stake for both teams, in the BCS, the national championship picture and in the SEC. There is a lot of luggage in this game."

Georgia coach Mark Richt isn't sure if this is the Bulldogs' biggest game, but he knows well what it means for the Tigers.

"To me, Auburn's got a lot more riding on it," Richt said. "They have a legitimate shot to play for the national championship if they win it.

"If we win it, we may not even play in the SEC championship game. But it's still very big for us. We're playing for possibilities, and they're playing for more real, tangible things."

Georgia running back Thomas Brown sits on the bench in the final moments of the Bulldogs' 24-6 loss to Auburn.

It's hard to tell if that pressure is an advantage or disadvantage for Auburn, which beat Tennessee and LSU in its only other games against ranked teams.

But neither of those games approached this magnitude for a program gunning for its first SEC title since 1989. Auburn won its only national championship in 1957.

Auburn players and coaches have become adept at downplaying the stakes publicly, but it's awfully hard this time.

"In the back of our minds, we know it's bigger than just another game," quarterback Jason Campbell said.

Safety Will Herring called it "the biggest game of the year," topping even next weekend's regular-season finale at Alabama.

"The Alabama game will be here when it gets here but Auburn- Georgia is one of the longest rivals in the south," Herring said. "With that and all this hype stacked on top of it, it's going to be an exciting game to watch.

"Games like this are what dreams are made of. People are going to remember this game for a long time."

That's because they don't happen all that often for the Tigers. This is only the 12th time two top-10 teams have squared off in Auburn. The Tigers are 4-6-1 in such games, including a 23-0 loss to Southern California in last year's opener.

This game also is reminiscent of the 1983 showdown, when third- ranked Auburn beat No. 4 Georgia 13-7 in Athens after winning two straight top-10 games at home.

Auburn coach Tommy Tuberville doesn't want his players sweating the high stakes too much.

"We are going to play a good football game, but we don't want to take the fun out of it by worrying every minute about playing this game," Tuberville said. "We need to worry about getting better, going out and having fun and focusing on what we are doing.

"You can't worry about all the things around it."

Because he won't be on the playing field, Housel can savor all the trappings a bit more.

"If you want to be one of the big boys, you've got to play the big boys," he said. "If you want to be a champion, you've got to play games like this."

Georgia vs. Auburn: a game with everything

JOHN ZENOR, November 12, 2004

This Georgia-Auburn game has it all: star quarterbacks, stingy defenses, talented running backs and high stakes.

It's got No. 3 Auburn trying to remain in the national

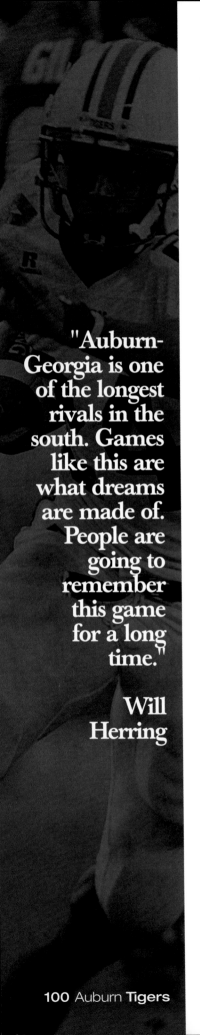

"Auburn-Georgia is one of the longest rivals in the south. Games like this are what dreams are made of. People are going to remember this game for a long time."

Will Herring

championship hunt and avenge losses the last two years to one of its biggest rivals, and No. 8 Georgia jockeying for a spot in the Bowl Championship Series.

It's also one of the most venerable rivalries, a series so competitive the teams are separated by only 17 points in 107 meetings.

"I don't think it gets any better than what it's going to be on Saturday," Auburn quarterback Jason Campbell said.

Not since 1983 have Georgia and Auburn met when both were ranked in the Top 10, and it had only happened one other time, in 1971.

Other than the BCS system itself, this could be the Tigers' biggest remaining hurdle for a national championship shot.

They are 9-0 and only LSU has come close in six league games. Auburn is scoring more points than any other SEC team and allowing fewer, giving up only one rushing touchdown.

"I don't know what I can say about Auburn other than that they're undefeated for a real good reason," Georgia coach Mark Richt said.

And with only a 19-14 loss to Tennessee marring their record, the Bulldogs (8-1, 6-1) are impressive in their own right.

A big challenge for Richt and Auburn coach Tommy Tuberville is finding a weakness on the other team. There aren't many.

Here's one possibility: Georgia has allowed 10 touchdown passes while snagging a league-low four interceptions. Auburn defensive coordinator Gene Chizik has considered replacing cornerback Montae Pitts, who was beaten for a 64-yard touchdown against Mississippi.

However, both defenses wreak plenty of havoc with their pass rush. Auburn leads the league with 32 sacks, Georgia is third with 25. The game also boasts the SEC's three leaders in sacks–Georgia's David Pollack and Auburn's Stanley McClover and Quentin Groves.

Georgia's David Greene, who missed

Monday's practice with a virus, became major college football's winningest quarterback with victory No. 40 last week against Kentucky. Tuberville called Greene perhaps the most consistent quarterback in SEC history.

Greene and Campbell are the league's top-rated passers, throwing 30 combined touchdown passes against a paltry three interceptions.

"It's not going to be a thing where it's Jason Campbell vs. David Greene," said Campbell, who called this the best defense Auburn has faced. "It's Auburn vs. Georgia."

There's also Thomas Brown and Danny Ware vs. Ronnie Brown and Carnell Williams.

All four rank in the league's Top 10 in rushing, forming perhaps the league's top two tailback duos. Georgia's Thomas Brown is expected to get the starting nod over fellow freshman Ware, who is coping with a sprained right knee and ankle.

Georgia handed the Tigers two of their toughest losses the past two seasons. Last year, the Bulldogs dominated in a 26-7 victory. Two years ago, Greene's late touchdown pass to Michael Johnson on fourth-and-15 won the game.

"With what both of us are ranked and all the national media hype, it's going to get played up as that kind of game," Campbell said. "It's a big rivalry game for us every year so I don't think that's going to add to the intensity too much."

No. 3 Auburn 24, No. 8 Georgia 6

RALPH D. RUSSO, November 14, 2004

Auburn appealed to the poll voters with a dominant performance that left coach Tommy Tuberville with little reason to give a stump speech.

The Tigers' 24-6 victory Saturday over No. 8 Georgia said it all.

Auburn players from left; Jay Ratliff (83), Tommy Jackson (58) Anthony Mix (9) and Mayo Sowell (57) celbrate with the fans after defeating Georgia.

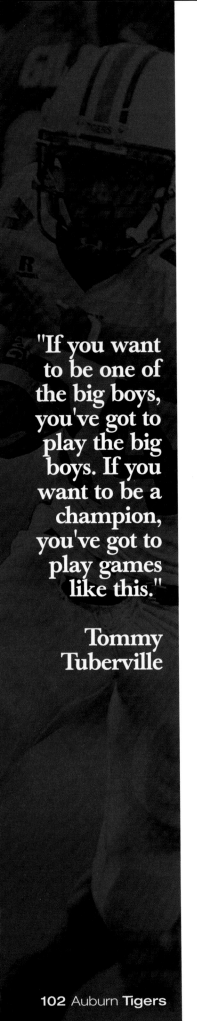

"If you want to be one of the big boys, you've got to play the big boys. If you want to be a champion, you've got to play games like this."

Tommy Tuberville

"One thing I'd say: I'd hate to play us," Tuberville said. "I know the people will be fair when they vote. That's all we can ask."

Carnell Williams, Ronnie Brown combined for 260 total yards and each scored a touchdown for the third-ranked Tigers, who may have earned the boost they needed in the Bowl Championship Series standings.

Auburn (10-0, 7-0 Southeastern Conference) was third in both polls and in the BCS standings behind Southern California and Oklahoma this week. The Tigers knew a big performance against the Bulldogs would go a long way toward convincing voters in The Associated Press media poll and coaches poll that they're better than the second-ranked Sooners, no matter what Oklahoma does in its last three games.

If Auburn can move past the Sooners in the polls, it should be able to move past them in the BCS standings. The top two teams in the final BCS standings will play in the Orange Bowl for the national championship.

"It's going to be hard not to vote for us," Williams said.

Indeed.

At least one voter said he was impressed.

"I've been voting them high," Georgia coach Mark Richt said. "I think they are one of the best, if not the best team in the country."

The 108th meeting between the SEC's oldest rivals was also the third time the Tigers and Bulldogs (8-2, 6-2) were both ranked in the top 10 when they met. But Auburn turned one of the most anticipated games ever played at Jordan-Hare Stadium into rout.

Auburn's dynamic tailback tandem of Williams and Brown did it all offensively.

"Awesome," Tuberville said. "You can't defense them. You just can't do it."

Williams ran 19 times for 101 yards and caught four passes for 20 yards. He also threw a TD pass and returned a punt 40 yards to set up Brown's 15-yard touchdown reception in the fourth quarter that made it 24-0.

Brown ran for 51 yards and caught seven passes for 88.

Georgia went scoreless for 57 minutes,

before David Greene hit Leonard Pope with a 6-yard TD pass with 2:13 left.

Auburn's defense held the Bulldogs to 279 yards and came up with two key takeaways deep in its own territory.

The second turnover came in the third quarter with Georgia trailing 17-0, but threatening to make it a game. Greene found Reggie Brown for what would have been a first down inside the Auburn 20, but safety Junior Rosegreen hammered Brown, causing a fumble that Will Herring scooped up for the Tigers.

Brown stayed down for several minutes after the helmet-to-helmet hit before slowly walking off. He missed the rest of the game with a concussion.

Greene was 15-for-22 for 159 yards and an interception. He also lost in an opponents stadium for just the second time in 17 games in his stellar career.

Auburn's West Coast offense gave Georgia a variety of looks, mixed plays masterfully and used Ronnie Brown and Williams every way they could on the way to a 17-0 halftime lead.

"They came out and did bootlegs, options and a lot of different things," Georgia defensive end David Pollack said. "They didn't really put themselves in bad predicaments."

The Tigers took a 7-0 lead on their first possession, completing an 80-yard march by running the option from the 1. Quarterback Jason Campbell waited until he was in the arms of a defender before pitching to Williams, who walked in for his 44th career TD, one shy of Bo Jackson's school record.

The Tigers got tricky again in the second quarter, sending Williams on what looked like a sweep right. Instead, he floated a soft pass to a wide-open Anthony Mix, who went 29 yards for a 14-0 lead.

Williams said the play always works in practice.

"When coach called that play, I said, 'Mix, touchdown. Let's get ready to celebrate,'" Williams said.

While Williams and Brown did the major

damage, Campbell directed the show. The SEC's top-rated passer completed 18 of 22 passes for 189 yards.

Georgia had a couple of opportunities to break through in the first half against the second-stingiest scoring defense in the nation, but failed to convert.

The best one came in the second quarter, when Pollack blocked a punt in Auburn territory. But Carlos Rogers picked off Greene's pass in the end zone, just the second interception the left-hander had thrown this season.

The Tigers still have two tough tests left, at Alabama next week and in the SEC title game on Dec. 4, most likely against Tennessee.

"I think there are some things for us to do," Tuberville said, "to maybe win a few more voters."

Tuberville goes from hot seat to hot commodity

JOHN ZENOR, November 15, 2004

Uh oh, the questions about Tommy Tuberville's job are starting to trickle in on Iron Bowl week again.

Only this time they're dealing with whether the Auburn coach will leave for some other job, which seems unlikely.

Last season, Tuberville entered the Alabama game thinking he was on the verge of being fired.

"It was tough because we thought it was over," Tuberville said. "It was a real tough scenario to go through."

Imagine how tough it would have been had he known that his bosses at Auburn were in Kentucky courting Louisville's Bobby Petrino two nights before the Tigers' biggest rivalry game. That revelation became public a few days after the game, and the backlash led Auburn officials to ask Tuberville to stay put. He agreed, and his players remain grateful.

"I always respected him. I respect him even more now for staying with us, even though they plotted to get him out of here," receiver Courtney Taylor said. "It takes a bigger man to stay here and face everything that went on down here during that time. I love the man."

Incidentally, the Tigers somehow managed to ignore the distractions and beat Alabama 28-23—starting their current 12-game winning streak. Normally, beating Alabama leads to raises and contract extensions for Auburn coaches—not an attempted coup, led by then-interim President William Walker.

The Sunday before last year's game, Tuberville instructed his players to ignore the rumors. This Sunday, he told them to forget about the "bowls and polls."

Clearly, Tuberville and the Tigers, who share the No. 2 ranking with Oklahoma but are third in the Bowl Championship Series standings, are dealing with different issues this year—like being on the brink of playing for a national title.

And here's a new one. Tuberville has been asked if he would be interested in the Miami Dolphins' coaching vacancy, since he broke into the major college ranks as an assistant with the Miami Hurricanes.

"I'm not a pro guy," Tuberville said. "I do not enjoy pro football. I like college football."

There's no bigger rivalry in the sport than Auburn-Alabama.

"It's for the fans that live for it for 365 days," Tuberville said. "The players and coaches did a great job last year under the circumstances."

Circumstances, he adds quietly, that were "very difficult."

Now, Auburn is a win shy of completing a perfect SEC regular season. The last two teams to do that—Tennessee in 1998 and Florida in 1996—both won national titles. The Tigers still must beat Alabama, win the SEC championship game and make up ground in the BCS standings to keep that trend going.

It's still worlds away from the position Tuberville was in a year ago.

"He turned everything around," Taylor said. "That's just a wonderful feeling. You go out every day and talk about players having your back. But at the same time, in the back of your mind, you know your coach has got your back. It's a great feeling."

	Georgia	Auburn
First Downs	15	21
3rd-Down Efficiency	5-13-38%	3-9-33%
4th-Down Efficiency	1-1-100%	0-1-0%
Total net yards	279	404
Net yards rushing	85	186
Net yards passing	194	218
Penalties-yards	8-68	5-45
Time of Possession	26:45	33:15

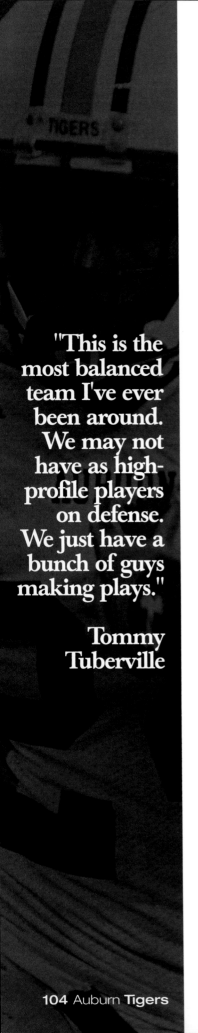

"This is the most balanced team I've ever been around. We may not have as high-profile players on defense. We just have a bunch of guys making plays."

Tommy Tuberville

No. 2 Auburn 21, Alabama 13

November 20, 2004

Auburn rides balanced attack to impressive win

JOHN ZENOR, November 15, 2004

Tommy Tuberville dug deep into his past to make a case for co-No. 2 Auburn as national champion.

Leaning back in a chair Saturday after his team's 24-6 domination of No. 11 Georgia, Tuberville compared these Tigers to the three title teams he helped coach with the Miami Hurricanes.

"This is the most balanced team I've ever been around," Tuberville said, making his pitch in the press box well after his postgame news conference. "We may not have as high-profile players on defense. We just have a bunch of guys making plays."

Indeed, the Tigers (10-0, 7-0 Southeastern Conference) displayed a relentless running game, a precision passing attack and a defense that easily bested one of the league's top offenses. The result was a move into a tie for No. 2 with Oklahoma in The Associated Press poll Sunday.

Georgia coach Mark Richt left Jordan-Hare Stadium impressed.

"I don't think there was a lack of fight or anything like that," Richt said. "We got out-executed, we got outcoached, and we got outplayed."

As a result, Auburn enters the Iron Bowl game Saturday at Alabama (6-4, 3-4) with a perfect record for the first time since 1993, when the team was on probation and ineligible for postseason play.

Before that, it hadn't happened since 1971.

The Tigers, who will have a rematch against either Tennessee or Georgia in the SEC championship game, are searching for a national title—and a nickname. After all, they started the season at No. 17 and weren't even picked to win the SEC West.

"This team's going to have be called something," Tuberville said. "They lay it on the line every week. They keep their focus, they're consistent and they're dang fun to watch."

Hard to stop, too. Auburn's trio of offensive stars makes sure of that.

Carnell Williams, Ronnie Brown and Jason Campbell all had big games against Georgia's defense. Campbell was never sacked by one of the league's top pass rushing teams, thanks to a combination of strong blocking, rollouts and quick throws to Brown and Williams out of the backfield.

"I would hate to be calling defenses on the other side," said Tuberville, a former defensive coordinator.

Auburn running back Carnell Williams drives through the Alabama defense.

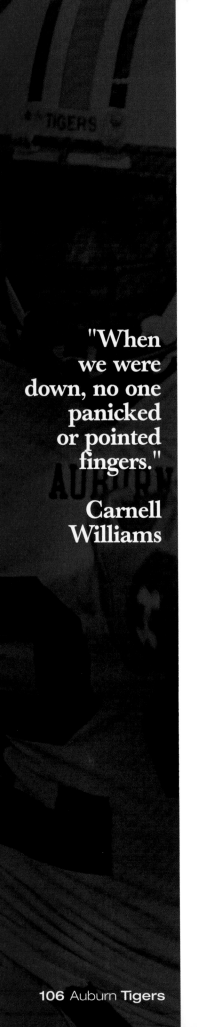

"When
we were
down, no one
panicked
or pointed
fingers."

Carnell
Williams

The defense harried Georgia's normally unflappable David Greene into a mediocre day. He was 15-of-22 for 159 yards and a touchdown but was picked off once in the end zone by Carlos Rogers and was sacked twice.

"They mixed a lot of things up that we really weren't ready for," Georgia receiver Fred Gibson said. "Every time we tried to go deep, they had the safety come up.

"Every time we tried to hit the middle of the field, one of the linebackers just came out and messed everything up. They did a whole lot of disguises."

The key, said Travis Williams, was "speed and not sitting back and letting him throw."

"We watched film and didn't see a lot of guys come after him," Williams said. "They just sit back and play scared, and he just eats them alive. We said if he's going to beat us, he's got to show us that he's that good to beat us."

Auburn players have mostly maintained they pay scant attention to the Bowl Championship Series and the polls. Cornerback Carlos Rogers isn't shying away from admitting he's spent plenty of time checking out the competition.

"At the beginning, we had a long, long season to go and we couldn't really pay attention to that," Rogers said. "But during our bye week, I won't lie to you, I watched the Oklahoma and USC games. I listened to the talk shows and watched (College Sports Southeast) and ESPN.

"They were talking about our defense, like can we stop the run? What did Georgia get, 85 yards?"

Travis Williams is hoping this performance convinces skeptics that Auburn has a championship caliber team.

"All season everyone has been telling us that we had not won a statement game," he said. "We wanted to make a statement and I think we did that."

Russo on Football: Who's No. 2? Auburn or Oklahoma

RALPH D. RUSSO, November 15, 2004

Auburn made its case on the field—and off—and enough voters were swayed.

The Tigers moved up to No. 2 in The Associated Press Top 25 on Sunday, but they're not alone. Auburn and Oklahoma now share the spot behind No. 1 Southern California in the media poll.

And they're only separated in the coaches poll by two points, with the Sooners holding the slim advantage.

The next thing to change will be the Bowl Championship Series standings, which come out Monday.

The annual debate about the BCS is about to reach a fever pitch. With three weekends of football left before the postseason matchups are determined, the chances of three major conference teams finishing unbeaten is a distinct possibility.

USC will play in the Orange Bowl for the BCS title on Jan. 4 with little protest if it wins its remaining two games.

As for the Tigers and Sooners, with two wins each, one will be on the way to Miami while the other is left to wonder why a 12-0 record and a major conference championship wasn't good enough.

This much is clear: If USC, Oklahoma and Auburn all run the table, a team deserving a shot at the national championship isn't going to get it. Nice job, BCS.

Auburn and Oklahoma each received 1,536 points in the latest AP poll. The Tigers got six first-place votes and the Sooners received eight. Last week, Oklahoma led Auburn by 43 and had 10 first-place votes to the Tigers' three.

Auburn made a convincing case Saturday against Georgia, beating the Bulldogs 24-6. It was Auburn's ninth victory of the season by

Auburn quarterback Jason Campbell ooks for a receiver during the first quarter against Alabama in the Iron Bowl.

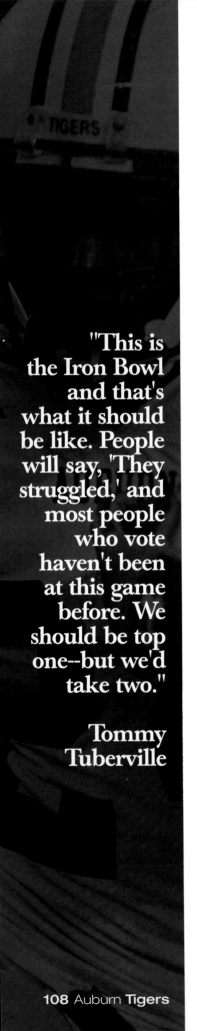

"This is the Iron Bowl and that's what it should be like. People will say, 'They struggled,' and most people who vote haven't been at this game before. We should be top one—but we'd take two."

Tommy Tuberville

at least two touchdowns.

"I haven't talked much about the BCS until this point," Auburn coach Tommy Tuberville said Saturday. "We had to get over this hump because of how good that team (Georgia) is."

Now, Tuberville is ready to talk about the BCS.

He made those comments not at the postgame news conference, but during an impromptu post-postgame news conference in the pressbox at Jordan-Hare Stadium. Tuberville admittedly dropped by to do a little lobbying.

Who knows whether it helped? It's doubtful that he could have said anything that was more persuasive than his team's stellar performance.

The Sooners beat Nebraska 30-3 on Saturday night, but it was their close calls the previous two weeks against Oklahoma State and Texas A&M that left the voters questioning Oklahoma's credentials.

The Sooners beat the Cowboys by three and the Aggies by seven, playing poor defense in each game.

Despite the struggles, Oklahoma's resume stacks up well with Auburn's.

Both are 10-0 with three victories against ranked opponents.

The Tigers have been winning more decisively, by an average of 25 points. The Sooners average margin is 16.8, but so far they've played a tougher schedule.

The Tigers' nonconference slate served up three cupcakes—Louisiana-Monroe, The Citadel and Louisiana Tech—making their push for the top spot difficult.

"Everybody's talking about catching Oklahoma," Tuberville said Sunday. "I don't understand how USC's gotten so far ahead of everybody else."

Oklahoma's nonconference schedule at least offered a couple of solid teams in Bowling Green and Oregon to go along with pushover Houston.

"Strength of schedule is important, but it's also how you are playing," Tuberville said.

"It's not like we've been winning by two or three points. We've been pretty much naming our score."

Since beating LSU 10-9 in September, Auburn has been running roughshod through the Southeastern Conference, including a 34-10 win at Tennessee.

Knowing style points count, Tuberville left his top defenders in the whole way against Georgia, hoping to blank the Bulldogs.

Oklahoma did the same against Nebraska, but lost the shutout on a field goal on the final play of the game.

"It is funny how we find ourselves in these circumstances at the end of games," Oklahoma coach Bob Stoops said. "It really puts you in an odd position. I don't like being in that position. Unfortunately, the way things are these days, that's the way it is."

To Oklahoma's credit, those recent tight games came on the road against ranked Big 12 teams. And the Sooners' 12-0 win over Texas came on a neutral field.

Auburn goes on the road Saturday to face Alabama before a likely rematch with Tennessee in the SEC title game in Atlanta on Dec. 4.

Win those two and the Tigers won't have to answer any questions about their schedule strength.

Oklahoma's remaining schedule is easier with Baylor and the Big 12 title game in Kansas City on Dec. 4 against one of weaklings from the North division, which doesn't bode well for the Sooners if Auburn wins out.

Or the BCS, which for all its tweaks and revisions is again on its way to solving nothing.

No. 2 Auburn 21, Alabama 13

JOHN ZENOR, November 21, 2004

Jason Campbell looked every bit the Heisman Trophy contender and No. 2 Auburn certainly played like a national championship contender—at least in the second half.

The Tigers' 21-13 victory over Alabama wound up as a survival contest instead of a hoped-for statement game, and left coach Tommy Tuberville lobbying for his team.

"This is the Iron Bowl and that's what it should be like," Tuberville said. "People will say, 'They struggled,' and most people who vote haven't been at this game before."

Still, the question is will an impressive final 30 minutes be enough to cancel out a 6-0 halftime deficit and lackluster start in the minds of poll voters. The Tigers (11-0, 8-0 Southeastern Conference) were tied for No. 2 with Oklahoma in the AP Top 25, but third in the Bowl Championship Series standings behind second-place Oklahoma, which beat Baylor 35-0, and Southern California.

Again, Tuberville had strong opinions on the matter: "We should be top one—but we'd take two."

Instead of touting their dominance, the Auburn players pointed to their resilience—something they haven't needed much of this season.

"When we were down, no one panicked or pointed fingers," said tailback Carnell Williams, whose 44th touchdown run broke Bo Jackson's school record.

"We weren't concerned," said Campbell, who passed for most of his 224 yards after halftime and finished 18-of-24.

He then celebrated by waving an Auburn flag in front of the visiting fans section while several teammates stomped on a homemade Alabama banner. But their dream destination, the Orange Bowl, loomed over the celebration, with fans tossing about a dozen oranges onto the field.

Even the nation's top scoring defense ran into a little trouble late. Alabama (6-5, 3-5) drove 84 yards on 11 plays in the final minutes, scoring on Spencer Pennington's 18-yard pass to D.J. Hall with 1:26 left.

Courtney Taylor recovered the onside kick for the Tigers, who ran out the clock.

They completed their first perfect regular season since 1993, when the team was on probation. Auburn will get one more chance to make an impression with poll voters and computer programs against Tennessee in the SEC championship game on Dec. 4, but might need a loss from Oklahoma or USC to make the Orange Bowl.

The defense kept Auburn from serious trouble in the first half, holding the league's No. 1 running team to 50 yards on 31 carries and allowing only three points out of two first-and-goal situations for the Tide. "This thing could have been over at halftime if the defense hadn't shown up," Tuberville said.

Kenneth Darby, the SEC's second-leading rusher, was hampered by a strained abdominal muscle and sprained ankle and had just 19 yards on 14 carries.

Alabama has been outscored 104-20 in five Iron Bowls in Tuscaloosa, and has lost three straight meetings for the first time since Auburn won four in a row from 1986-89.

The Tigers finally looked like the team that has been dominating SEC teams most of the season in the second half, taking charge of the game.

"They hadn't really been in that situation all season," Tide linebacker Cornelius Wortham said. "They showed what type of team they were in the second half. They went into the half, took care of their Xs and Os and came out a different team."

Campbell hit Devin Aromashodu for a 51-yard pass down the left sidelines and Williams bounced outside for a 5-yard touchdown to cap a six-play, 80-yard drive to open the half.

Campbell hit Taylor for a 32-yard touchdown pass on third-and-17 on Auburn's next series to make it 14-6. Brown added a 2-yard TD plunge early in the fourth quarter.

Campbell was 8-of-9 for 143 yards in the third after passing for just 61 yards and an interception before the half against the nation's top pass defense.

Brown and Williams combined for just 96 rushing yards.

Fast starters all season, the Tigers came out looking out-of-sync, losing 4 yards on their first three series. Campbell had to burn timeouts on successive plays on the second series and it didn't get much better.

The Tigers slumped off the field after John Vaughn missed a 21-yard field goal as time expired on the half.

	Auburn	Alabama
First Downs	18	15
3rd-Down Efficiency	6-13-46%	3-14-21%
4th-Down Efficiency	1-2-50%	1-3-33%
Total net yards	298	276
Net yards rushing	74	50
Net yards passing	224	226
Penalties-yards	4-26	3-20
Time of Possession	32:47	27:13